PAPER KEEPER

RECOVERING MY STORY THROUGH CLUES LEFT BEHIND

BARBARA BECKWITH

Paperback ISBN: 979-8-9931087-2-8

www.barbarabeckwith.net

CONTENTS

INTRODUCTION

I'm fascinated by memory: by what we remember and what we forget, by what we think we've forgotten, but haven't. In preparation for this book, I spent countless hours going through piles of documents I had saved for decades, including journals, letters, and detailed trip logs. Reading words I had written throughout my life brought memories of all of those times flooding back—and proving to me that they never really did go away.

This project began in 2009 when my son Anthony asked me to write a detailed description of the jobs I've held throughout my life, as he had recently done for his two sons. Instead of a page or so of bulleted points for the jobs I held, I ended up writing more than 20 pages, working to make my job descriptions come alive and to weave in my evolving perspective on my own life.

As I looked back at the jobs I held, I saw how much I yearned to be a "real" job holder like my dad and like women who came after me that were unburdened by 1950s expectations. That yearning seesawed with the joy I found in writing: stories, letters, poems, diaries, articles, essays, travel logs.

THIRTY YEARS LATER, after Anthony finished writing a memoir of his own (*My Ride Through Life: A Cambridge Kid Finds Identity in Dirt Lots, City Schools, and Reggae Beats*), we realized that my "jobs description document" could be expanded to include other parts of my life: family, friends, travel, activism, aging—and so our collaboration began to turn a "list" into a narrative of one person's life: mine.

To do so, I've pulled out *my* strand from the deeply entwined life that my husband Jon and I have shared for 70 (so far) years, just as he did when he wrote his memoir, *Making Genes, Making Waves: A Social Activist in Science* (Harvard University Press, 2002). We each have our stories to tell.

Along the same lines, I would have loved to include every friend, neighbor, colleague, and activist who has been part of my life, but I've resisted for the sake of both their privacy and my story's brevity.

As I've been writing, I've caught my own flawed memories; I remembered my first typewriter being a Royal, but found an early account of my life that says it was an Underwood. I remembered visiting Spelman College but the back of my photos showed it was Fisk University.

Consider this account of my life as an invitation to whoever reads it to do the same with their life. Like kids curious about private parts would say to each other: "You show me yours, and I'll show you mine."

Paper scraps that I just can't throw away

1

"MY FUTURE AND I"

New York/New Jersey

My birth in 1937 gave my father Joe a slightly off-color story to tell his friends. He finally shared it with me when he was in his 80s and I was in my 50s, as we were gathering memories for an oral history of his early life.

The doctor had warned my parents that my birth could be problematic (feet first breech) and told my mother Marian that when she first felt contractions, she should get to the Presbyterian Hospital in Brooklyn as quickly as possible. Dad recounted to me in 1990 that:

> *Marian and I had just bought a car from [Mom's brother-in-law] Steve who was in the Chrysler business in Stroudsburg. He gave us the best price. I was very pleased with the car and had it parked right outside the house.*
>
> *When Marian realized it was about time, I went out to start the car. It wouldn't start. I panicked, and ran down the street and saw a parked car. I ran up to it and looked in and a couple was having intercourse.*

I said, "I'm so sorry." He said, "Goddamn it!" and so forth and was very upset. I apologized and said, "My wife is going to have a baby and I can't start my car. I need some help." Finally, he conceded and he and his girlfriend drove us to the hospital.

I said to the man, "I want your name and address to send you a gift." I sent this guy a very generous check, but I'll never forget the sadness in this guy's eyes: he was so upset that I had interrupted his sexual intercourse.

When I went home, I got back in the car and turned the ignition and it started—I was amazed. I had been so concerned that I'd done something wrong.

But that, of course, is just my father's side of the story. I saved a letter that my mother wrote to her sister Ruth six days after giving birth to me, where she recounted the facts of that 1937 night in Brooklyn that *she* found important:

At 11:30 pm, I felt a violent sudden pain and the water broke in a deluge. Joe immediately called the doctor, threw some perfectly incongruous clothes on me and we got out to the car. It sputtered and stopped in the middle of the crossing by our house—the gas seemed to register empty (it wasn't empty, but half full, we later discovered), so in a panic Joe pushed it off the street and ran down half a block to where a car was parked with a young Jewish couple in it.

In about one minute we were in that car driving at an awful rate through all the lights and getting to the hospital at 11:50. From then on, it was just about indescribable—at 12:14 am the baby was born—a breech birth which is supposed to be long and painful.

My mother had left out the detail of what the couple was

doing in the car, but did include the incongruity of the clothing that Dad had fetched for her, the couple's Jewish Identity, and the fact that my birth took little more than 20 minutes.

WHILE I WAS STILL AN INFANT, we moved from Brooklyn to Bellrose, Queens, and later to 118 Tullamore Road in Garden City, Long Island, one of America's first "planned communities." It had been founded by the Irish immigrant Alexander Turney Stewart, considered at the time to be the third richest man in the United States. At first he allowed only renters, not home buyers, until he was satisfied with their "family backgrounds" (as a way to exclude Jews and Blacks, perhaps?) Later, it was said that to live in Garden City, you had to be "Rich, Republican and Episcopal" (though we were none of those).

My Mother's Work

MY MOTHER WASN'T a career model for me—she could have been, except that I didn't know until recently that she'd ever worked at a paid job. Mom never shared that, before we were born, she had been an assistant supervisor of casework for the Brooklyn Children's Aid Society. After finishing two years post-graduate work at the New York School of Social Work, she had started, but never finished, her Master's degree in Social Work. Apparently, Mom's job at the Aid Society was to evaluate orphanages. I have one of her reports, which shows her concern at the paucity of "Negro orphanages." She notes that almost every orphanage she visited did not take "Negro children"—leaving many of them without good care. I recently found a 1947 letter accepting Mom's resignation from the Aid Society's board of trustees. This means that she must have held this position—probably unpaid—until I was about ten years old. How did I not know this?

I found a letter that explains Mom's decision not to pursue a career. She wrote her sister Ruth that she was very glad she'd gotten married and was "so very very glad it was to Joe" (she had almost married a rich Italian graduate student, named Freddi). She wrote about how she'd found in marriage "...a bond or an interdependency that I wanted so much more than independence or adventure or some alluring unknown." She then writes about *not* wanting to work:

> *I don't feel that an outstanding "career" would give me satisfaction, that the prestige or the salary would be worth the concentrated effort (and yet I'm enjoying my job particularly). I was offered the position of Supervisor of Care Work—it's the key position in our organization and I think that with lots of effort I could have fulfilled it. But I want to read what interests me as a layman in my off hours—I want places of work that I feel I can do with most genuine interest—instead of worrying about the total responsibility that I'd have otherwise. In short, I want to be just plain me, and feel the ease and mastery at being THAT—instead of straining to be more than I can with comfort.*

In a way, Mom was following the path that her mother, Mary Stokehill, took. Mary was a Sunday School teacher when she was young—likely a volunteer. She had been born in Leeds, England, married my Grandpa, had four children, but tragically died during the 1918 influenza epidemic when Mom was only eleven. The 1899-1908 diary of the grandmother I never had the chance to know ends with this entry about how she saw her role in life:

> *Now the problem that demands attention: how to be a good wife, a competent housekeeper, a good mother, and a helpful neighbor and friend.... I cannot stand alone and do it justice. So I ask God to come and be my strength and my guide. I know that if I let God answer He will say "As thy day, so thy strength be."*

Taking care of three children wasn't easy for my mother, especially because my father traveled constantly for his work as a development officer. My mother took care of all three of us, sometimes with hired help, but most of the time alone. At first, my father was the Director of Fundraising for the National Foundation for Infantile Paralysis, focusing on raising funds for the March of Dimes campaign to end infantile paralysis (polio). He then moved to the American Cancer Society and to the Council on Medical Aid to Education.

Each summer, the four of us—Mom, along with me and my sisters Linda and Joanne—all went to Henryville (a woodsy area in Pennsylvania's Pocono mountains) while Dad sweated away in New York City, making the long train ride to see us on the weekends. Our countryside summers supposedly kept us "safe" from the polio epidemic and we could swim, bike, and explore the woods with our many cousins while Mom socialized with her sisters. But the responsibility was wearying for her. Mom's gracefully written letters to my father (the letters addressed him as "Joie" or "Joey") showed her yearning for him, alongside her dedication to her three daughters and to her letter-writing, despite her exhaustion.

My parents felt that we should use our spare time in the summer either for reading or for enjoying the outdoors. We'd take out stacks of library books and I'd climb up large trees to spend hours reading in the crook of a branch. I spent so much time running over stony fields in bare feet that I could race shoeless to catch frisbees and baseballs—or my little sister. Yet my feet stayed so sensitive that I could feel the tickle of grass as they dangled off the back of the pickup truck, and the nibble of minnows as I fished in streams.

I was adept at climbing up not only trees, but also rocky cliffs and the metal bars that held up the swing set. My toes would splay out to grip the cold metal, while I used my arms for balance. The top of the jungle gym was just ten feet off the ground. The adults knew I wouldn't die if I fell, so they let me climb all I wanted. Everyone was amazed. My goal-oriented father thought I could be a circus performer.

I didn't particularly like high school sports (a requirement) but did love swimming, hiking, skiing, canoeing, tennis and learning to shoot a rifle (at a target across a field by the blueberry bushes). Being active in Henryville led to my finding pleasure in exercise as an adult: I would become a runner and regularly play tennis with my friend Gail Graves. I would become a rock-climber, whitewater canoeist, and winter-camper with friends. My husband Jon and I would also go on to backpack in just about every mountain range in the United States and explore the U.S. and Europe through self-guided bike-camping trips.

When I was in ninth grade, Dad was between jobs, so we lived for one delicious full year in Henryville. We were driven each day to the Stroudsburg schools, 11 miles away. I loved Spanish (I've always loved languages), botany (identifying by bark and leaves the names of the trees surrounding the school), the rifle club (I was president) and marching band (cousin Betsey and I both played flute at home and away football games). Experiencing the wooded area in all four seasons has been special to me all my life.

Once Dad found a new job, we moved back towards the city, landing in suburban Chatham, New Jersey. Chatham was just 25 miles outside of Manhattan but was (much like Garden City) mostly white and Protestant and was known as a "bedroom community," because the men would commute daily to their jobs in New York City. Our family had now moved twice, each time to a new state, where I would have to adjust to new schools and make new friends. Being a lively conversationalist, I was able to make friends quickly, but I also had the challenge of staying close to my girlfriends that I'd left behind. Telephone calls were considered too expensive, so letter writing became a critical way to stay in touch with the important people in my life.

"MY FUTURE AND I"

My sister Linda, father Joe, me, and mother Marian, Brooklyn, NY, c.1938

2

EARLY WRITING

When I was three or four, my mother overheard me telling myself a rambling rhythmical story about angels playing football and getting grass between their toes. I couldn't write yet, but my mother wrote down and saved this first babbled "poem." As soon as I learned to write, my parents bought me my own Underwood typewriter, probably so that they wouldn't have to type up my stories and poems. I wrote "novels" with many chapters. I think I must have been aware of racial and economic disparities because of what I chose to write about in elementary school. In one of my stories, a redheaded girl (like myself) makes friends with a "Negro girl" who was poor and worked on a plantation. In another, a redheaded girl like myself helps a boy find a lost valuable ring that his Mexican family needs because they are poor.

Mom was an encourager: she loved everything I wrote. Dad was goal-oriented: he saw talents and passions as projects always needing to be "worked on." Mom's positivity about my writing, I now realize, was because she, too, loved to write. When I went away to college, she and I exchanged letters more than once a week. After she died, I found charming short stories she'd written, so she may have wanted to publish her writing, as I eventually did get to do.

Mom was part of a "Great Books" reading group for years. She "talked with" the assigned classics by penciling comments in the margins. In a book of sixteenth century philosopher Montaigne's personal essays, she wrote this mix of anecdotes and ruminations: "Re-read," "POWs," "What about segregation laws?" "Allergies," "UN." She made five approving checkmarks next to this passage of Montaigne's (which showed how she and I think alike):

> *These are my own particular opinions and fancies, and I deliver them as only what I myself believe, and not for what is to be believed by others. I have no other end in this writing but only to discover myself, who, also, shall, peradventure, be another thing tomorrow, if I chance to meet any new instruction to change me. I am myself the matter of my book.*

Decades after my mother passed I wrote similar thoughts in my journal:

> *I am an expert only on myself. I couldn't even write from Jon's point of view, which is inextricably involved in the inner thoughts that AREN'T said. I know how Jon talks and acts and how he says he feels and thinks. But the rest—the web of fantasies and worries and pictures streaming through his mind, I don't know. I don't even know how he sees me.*

Just this year, I found Mom's college freshman essay "Inventory of My Life." It describes her upbringing, which involved much praying (Presbyterian) and often feeling inferior and unpopular, but then gradually sensing her ability to be creative and thoughtful. She wrote about this change:

Began, through letter-writing in particular—to express spontaneity, fresh thoughts, self-confidence—life. Interested in my own imagination, in expressing in little [illegible word] forms, with cool delight, the feelings I used to get moody about, of people not getting the me of me for example. Feeling myself peculiar, [illegible word] between certain people and myself different from what others knew, making them realize I was more alive than I could express to what I heard and saw.

~

In my elementary school writings, you can see my future profession bubbling up: I remember writing a "class poem" at the end of fifth grade, thinking up a funny blurb about each of the dozens of students in the class.

My teacher's fifth grade report on me shows what I was good at—and what I wasn't so good at:

Reading—excellent—Barbara reads with interest and has a good understanding of the material. She has a very well developed mind and she takes advantage of every situation which will help her improve it. Her creative ability in story writing is outstanding. Barbara needs to be more conscious of spelling. The results of her daily work in arithmetic are satisfactory. She has contributed a great deal to the entire group.

- M. Atkinson, 1949

I also wrote on my own—for myself. I reported in my 1947 diary that: "Yesterday I started my newspaper and I'm quite far on it now. And I'm having a poem or a play soon." Mom encouraged me to write a poem to Dad on his birthday, at Christmas, on Father's Day. I still have some of those "dad-as-hero" poems. Gwen Williams, who babysat for us when she was a teenager wrote me a letter in 1952: "I loved your last letter. Did you ever think of being a writer, Bobby? You know how to express yourself so well."

In Junior high school, I wrote about my English teacher, who we students liked because she liked *us*, despite out shenanigans:

She put up with a lot. Like the time we gave her an Esquire calendar when she said she wanted a calendar with big figures. Or the time we threw erasers up on the lights and smelled up the whole room. Or when we put perfume in her ink bottle. Or when we all beat on our desks at 9:20 making the math class downstairs complain of the roar.

In my junior high school years, I had international "penpals" which at that time was a way for kids to get to know kids from other countries (Aileen from Renfrewshire, Scotland, Denis Lagat from Villeneuve-sur-Bellot, France).

I wrote poems, accounts of trips, and judgmental descriptions of each of my friends and relatives—and of myself. Starting when I was ten, I wrote daily in a diary, and continued, as an adult, journaling about my experiences and feelings:

I am self-centered and acquisitive and often deceitful and far from perfect, but I am also pleasant and fun and natural and never will be "a phony."

Also:

I am tired of boys and of figuring things and people out. I want to be detached from mingling with human relations and lives —I want to get away with art or something.

I may have been 13 when I had an assignment to write an autobiography, including a section titled "My Future and I" about what I planned to do in my life. My response shows that I pictured myself as a job holder (not as a homemaker):

Perplexing problem, one's future. I suppose I should have an ambition by now, as most everyone does. But I don't. Oh, I've had many ambitions, the usual ones of being a teacher, actress, veterinarian, secretary, linguist, ballet dancer, artist, writer and owner of a dog kennel.

Most of these were soon squelched as a future profession by such things as: almost getting sick when Bonny [our dog] had her teeth knocked out, hearing that few teachers marry, doing a messy job at one-fingered typing, failing to get parts in school plays, having a poem I wrote rejected from The American Girl, getting only average marks in Art, and knowing only one language—Spanish.

I still wish to continue in Art, writing and other "dreams" but only as hobbies.... I am going to college, but that is just about all I am certain of. Maybe I can figure out what I am suited for there.

What strikes me about my ambitions is my assumption that teachers don't get married (women teachers, at least). But up at least until the 1950s teachers *were* expected to remain single (they would be called "old maids"). Some school systems fired women who married, on the grounds that a pregnant teacher would look "unseemly" and cause students to ask questions that no teacher should have to answer.

In high school I wrote a sonnet that my teacher thought was brilliant. She wanted me to keep writing them. But I wrote in my diary:

I thought my sonnet was a jumbled mess—I started with a broad idea and had to narrow it considerably to fit 14 lines. In narrowing it, I ruined the continuity and the fact that I mixed carefully chosen words with words that just fit in, bothered me considerably. I was not as satisfied as I usually am after a lot of hard struggle.

Despite my lack of satisfaction, the people around me encouraged me to write, allowing that creative part of me to keep blossoming. My English teacher released me from class in my last semester so that I could simply spend my time doing what I loved: writing.

Other Art Forms

In my early teens, art was a minor passion. I would paint outdoor scenes, inspired by my Uncle Stevie's bucolic oil paintings and by another Henryville artist, Joe McIntosh. I used only watercolor, applying it with my fingers instead of a brush. I liked the visceral feel of directly applying the paint. Mom drove me to an art class in Stroudsburg where I happily drew alongside adults. Years later, I sketched gothic churches and, after college, took art classes in Boulder, Colorado, while making repeated visits to an exhibit of modern art there. I even considered applying to MFA art programs.

I played the flute in an orchestra or band from elementary school through high school, and I enjoyed playing ensembles with my cousin Betsey (flute), my Aunt Bibsy (viola, piano, accordion), and my Uncle Stevie (bass), or recorders with Betsey. Later, my college "Music 101" course almost ruined classical music for me by forcing me to analyze and memorize what I just wanted to enjoy. I still struggle to erase that analytic requirement when I hear music, usually by simply recalling my Aunt Bibsy's love of music for itself.

World Events

I WAS JUST four in 1941 when Japan attacked American ships at Pearl Harbor and the United States entered World War II. Dad wasn't drafted, I assume because of his age (he was 35) and being responsible for two children at the time. He was asked instead to direct the Department of War's Manpower program at Sperry Gyroscope, whose mission was to recruit workers (including women and Blacks) at the war materials plant.

I remember that we bought "war bonds" and instead of butter, used margarine, which came in bags and a red button of color that I'd massage into the margarine. We saved "silver paper" (aluminum foil) by rolling it into balls. My father says that my mother "was sure that the Germans were going to come and bomb our place. She would put you and Linda in a closet."

I was five when the war ended in 1945 after America dropped atom bombs on Hiroshima and Nagasaki. Soon after, President Roosevelt died. I will never forget my father's serious tone when he came down the stairs and into our basement "rec room," where I was playing, to tell me about the president's death. At some point I saw pictures of victims of our Hiroshima and Nagasaki bombing and of concentration camp victims and survivors: images that are seared into my memory.

I was ten years old when the Korean War started. After the U.S. sent troops there, I heard whispered stories about the son of my parents' friends, who had been captured and put into a prisoner of war camp—and that he and his buddies had killed another U.S. soldier who was colluding with "the enemy." Later, when I was 17, we watched the 1955 McCarthy hearings on "Communists" and Dad was furious with McCarthy. I don't remember anything being said at home about civil rights at the time. My heightened awareness and pull to activism was still years away.

c. 1948. I was most happy when outdoors - notice the bandage on my knee

MY OWN MOMMY

I'm writing this poem on mothers day
IT's a day for mommy's to relax and play.
IF i had a problem,you'd understand too
Because youre like ne,and i'm like you.
You work very hard,to keep the houde clean
So i'll give you a kiss,'cuse you're my little dream.
I don't want money,so i'll give it a shove
I just want mommy and her mommy like love.
I wouldn't marry Peter, I wouldn't marry Tom
But if mommy was a little boy,then i'd marry mom.
I'll love my mommy,until I die
But I just have to kiss you right now,
so I gotta say good-bye

Some very early writing, using my Underwood typewriter

To watch the white and fleecy clo
go soaring, flying by ~~through the sky~~
This is the sky that sends us rain
Which gets us soping wet,
It sends the frost, the cold, the snow
That makes our parents fret.
It sends the wind which blows the sk
And makes the girls regret
That they'd ever gone out shopping
That they'd ever walked the pet.
It gives us all our blizzards
Or our scorching heat, and yet,
The sky is a creation
And that, I ~~won't~~ can't forget

A handwritten poem

Bill Brady and I won best sportsmanship awards—I was on the lacrosse team. Chatham High School, 1955

3
JOBS AND "STATUS"

Writing was my passion from an early age, but I also thrived on "doing stuff"—talking things over, sharing ideas, making plans, accomplishing goals. I loved group projects like organizing a club with my friends or a neighborhood circus (our $6.01 profit went to a charity; I still have its letter of thanks). In Henryville, my cousins and I organized summertime "entertainments" (we'd charge a fee and donate all the money to the Fresh Air Fund). I did occasional "teenager jobs," like babysitting, for 50 cents an hour. In Henryville, my cousin Betsey and I set up a house-cleaning business (I have our price list somewhere). I remember cleaning one very large house on a very hot day.

But I didn't *have* to have a job. I think that it was actually a point of pride for my father that he could support us—that we didn't *have to* work—perhaps partly because he'd *had* to work to help support the family. Dad's general contractor father, Walker Shutt, was killed by a train as he was directing road work near the railroad tracks and as a result, the family became impoverished.

At age eleven, to help support his mother and his two sisters, my father trimmed pine trees for boll weevil. In describing his work at MacAlevy's Fort, where 15 to 20 boll weevil workers slept in cots each night in an old farmhouse filled with wildlife, Dad recounted, "I have killed more rattlesnakes and copperheads than the average person." He was also "hired out" each summer (ages 12-19) to work on farms where he milked cows and drove teams of horses with plough and harrow; he briefly worked 6am-6 pm in a silk mill at age fifteen; he dug ditches and handled dynamite at age sixteen. At seventeen, he climbed poles to run the area's first electrical wires.

I once wrote a poem entitled "To My Father," which I never shared with him:

You drove work horses four abreast
They ran away but you held on
Your father died and you became the Man
You threw your sisters' beaux out—they eloped
You fire-fought, made bricks, and worked on farms
Taught kids older than you in just one room
You got to college with your brawn
And climbed up to Manhattan with your charm
And then you met my mother, rich and clever
She teased your backward speech away forever
You married, had us, vowed to teach us right
You brought us up in "bedroom cities"
Safe and green and pretty
And I dream now of hauling hay
or carrying stone
or driving trucks
or tending bars
or selling gas
or breaking trails
The best of you I never got

My mother saw our growing up years not as a time for work, but as time we ought to be spending on school and reading and in the outdoors, and on growing as people. Fortunately, my parents didn't have the usual worries about college tuition for us three kids ($500 a year back then) because my grandfather had left an educational fund for each of his grandchildren.

Despite having grown up in a family of little means, Grandpa Hunter worked his way up to eventually become president of the Schrader Valve Company in Brooklyn—and made smart real estate moves. As a result, Mom had been raised in a household that included maids, a cook, and a chauffeur. Mom may have been drawn to Dad in part because his upbringing was the opposite of hers: he'd been raised in a rural village and in a home with no books except the Bible. Dad and Mom were also attracted to each in part because they suffered similar losses: he lost his father when he was just eleven, the same age that Mom was when her mother died.

My father had always been keenly aware of, and eager for, status (having been raised without it), while my mother raised us to appreciate everyone—except "snobbish people"—probably as a rejection of her own high-status upbringing. Mother raised me to not be competitive, while my father liked to compete. Dad (who was a wrestler and football player in college) once told me:

> *I like to win. It was a desire to excel more than winning. To be superior to others. I get a certain satisfaction in playing better than someone else. It's a measurement of your capacity. I wasn't very good at tennis but I liked to play at the net, up at the front where the action is—I liked the extra heat.*

As for competition, the only award *I* ever got in high school was for "sportsmanship"—I was never a sore loser, probably because I didn't care about winning. I don't know if this was, in the long run, a good trait or not.

Since our "job" as kids was to have adventures and grow socially, in the summer of 1953—while other teens needed to take golf caddy or soda jerk jobs—Linda and I traveled across the country by train to California, where we went on a Sierra Club hiking trip. We stayed in Berkeley with our Aunt Ruth and Uncle Henry Colby (whose father had been one of the founders of the Sierra Club). They took us on a "training hike," to prepare our bodies and to break in our new boots, which still gave us blisters. Then we joined 80 hikers for a 20-day trip: about 160 miles, plus a side trip for those of us ambitious enough to climb Mt. Whitney, the highest mountain in the U.S. (outside of Alaska).

We had to carry daypacks only—mules carried our clothes and sleeping bags and "the commissary" made dinner for us hikers each night. Linda and I then came back by train, but stopped in Banff on the way back and stayed there overnight. We dealt with mishaps (I lost my travelers' checks) and enjoyed mini-adventures like meeting two sailors who took us out for the day.

The next summer (1954), Linda and I were American Friends Service Committee volunteers assigned to different towns in Mexico. Mine was a small farming town called Jicaltapec, which had dirt roads and carts, but no cars, and was reachable only by ferry. I taught art and recreation to the town's kids. It was my first "community organizing" experience.

I loved the children and adults I got to know, and the Spanish I learned that summer has stuck with me. I could clearly see through the "lazy Mexican" stereotype, writing home that the people I'd met were the most hard-working people I'd ever met. My positive view of Mexicans from that summer persists today. However, I suspect that for the wife of the married man who pursued me in Jicaltapec, the feeling was not mutual. I still have little slips of paper with song lyrics he gave me, as he serenaded me and then followed me to Mexico City. I was flattered, but also chagrined, knowing it was wrong.

At some point during high school, a youth group that I was part of had a "cultural exchange" trip to Fisk University in Nashville, Tennessee. The University was founded after Reconstruction out of the Fisk Free Colored School and was an HBCU (historically Black college or university). We stayed in the dormitories and attended some classes. One of the classes I remember was a philosophy class, where the back and forth between the students and the professor felt exciting to me. That experience made me realize how intellectually stimulating college could be and I never forgot that it was Black students who inspired me by those discussions.

A 1954 letter I wrote fto a high school chum shows that I was always examining myself and sharing my conflicts and dilemmas through writing:

> *I have to figure out what to do this summer. I want to get a job but at WHAT? I'm so dumb at everything. I'm not good enough for anything that requires typing. Lots of kids take summer babysitting jobs (I haven't the patience) or work in stores or are hostesses at restaurants. I'm about the only one who doesn't work.*

AFTER I GRADUATED from high school in 1955, Linda and I worked as unpaid summer "apprentices" at the Pocono Playhouse near Henryville. We painted sets, ran errands, and showed patrons to their seats (we got to see the shows for free). Theater did not, however, interest me: I'd wander off to read books, which made other volunteers think me lazy.

I started at Wellesley college that fall. On September 24, the men who murdered Emmett Till in Mississippi were acquitted and walked free. I have kept a copy of the Pocono Record from that day, because recovery from the worst flooding in Pennsylvania's history was still ongoing and the lake we swam in had been destroyed. Now, when I look at the front page, I see that the acquittal news shares top billing with news of the flood. I wonder if I'd been so focused back then on the local effects of the hurricane that the news of this terrible racist miscarriage of justice didn't even register.

The Psychic Space

I CHOSE to go to Wellesley College in large part because the campus was so beautiful. Another reason was that my family thought that I was "boy crazy" and so needed to attend a women's college. Such colleges, Hillary Clinton later wrote, gave students "the psychic space," and the opportunities, to lead, since all the clubs and other organizations were run by women.

I was excited by the new subjects I was studying, but I was clearly less prepared than "the private school kids." I tested well in the verbal parts of standardized tests, but this was in part because I'd always loved words so much: a favorite pastime of mine was to read the dictionary. My grades at Wellesley were mediocre (B's and C's, no A's). In my sophomore year, I worried that my mother's alumnae status had gotten me in to Wellesley and that maybe I wasn't really qualified to be there (that probably wasn't true, since I'd been accepted as well at Middlebury and Bennington, where I had no alumni connections). In a way, I was experiencing a downside of what was essentially "affirmative action" (in this case, "legacy admissions"): when the chips are down, you might question whether you belong in the school or are "up to the job."

As incoming freshmen, we were given a series of tests, including reading (I did well), speech (I was told to work on my "s"), and posture (I wasn't sent to "remedial posture" class). Decades later, it was revealed that our nude photos had been part of a notorious program at several Ivy League colleges. Many of our full nude photos were taken by W.H. Sheldon, a racist eugenicist, who claimed they were being used to assess posture and health; instead, he used them to "prove" that body measurements could predict intelligence and "moral worth." His collection of more than 20,000 photos was sealed by the Smithsonian Institution in 1995 and destroyed shortly thereafter. (It turns out that schools including Wellesley had been assessing incoming students' posture since the late 19th century.) While we sought knowledge, we were being groomed for wifehood.

DURING MY FOUR years of college, I was constantly writing to my mother, and I'm grateful that she saved those letters. Since I threw away all of my college notebooks and papers, these letters are the only existing record of my Wellesley experience:

In college, I wrote home with stunning frankness:

> *Don't expect a repeat of my first semester marks. I am doing very poorly. I don't know why. My reasons fluctuate between an inferiority complex, a natural lack of intelligence, lack of a specialization or a goal. Fear which turns to boredom which turns to a mental block (Music class), lack of someone to keep checking on me, a tendency to avoid thinking about unpleasant things like doing unpleasant homework (music listening assignments), and just plain laziness. I could never go to grad school with my marks, and here I am not doing anything about it.*

But over those four years, my self-criticism and fluctuating self-confidence were leavened by a passion for creative (if not analytical) writing. In my junior year, I wrote to my mother:

> *I told you once shame on you that you had built up my poetical abilities etc. and that when I got to college and realized I hadn't any it was a rude shock. I was wrong to be angry because if I believed I could write, I would probably sit down and do so. I will some day, in fact.*

I shall become the founder of the Pro City School of Poets: we shall immortalize street corners and eulogize the Automat.

My mother absorbed all my feelings, supporting me even when I blamed her, at one point, for my entering college not knowing about classical music, architecture, and other subjects my classmates all seemed familiar with. I confided with her freely, and with touches of self-analysis:

I'm reading Blake and he's hard but that doesn't matter. Molu and I had a talk about that today: the crux of it was that we are so busy learning that we aren't appreciating. I can lecture on Mrs Dalloway but if you were to ask me if I like it, I couldn't say, because I don't take time to react to it.

I occasionally found a perspective on what I knew or didn't know: "I guess one doesn't really find the truth, one just grows to see broader and more complicated views of things."

In college, we were expected to do volunteer work (while scholarship students *had* to work), so in 1957 I briefly volunteered to work with children at the Boston School for Blind Babies. I wrote to my mother criticisms of the staff (apparently I already was developing a teacher-to-be sensibility):

They don't seem to be making an effort to arouse the children's imaginations: they pat and hug but wouldn't it be better, if a boy begins to turn slowly to music, to encourage him to dance, or to get up and dance in a circle with him?

I also briefly campaigned for Adlai Stevenson and for a year tutored a woman from an Arab country (her name was Mrs. Habibi) who lived in Brookline but was expected to stay inside her house as her husband went off to study or work, making my visits a welcome break from the boredom.

My academic classes were fraught, but I enthusiastically

participated in physical activities because they gave me no worries. Haralyn Dubin and I were pals in the Wellesley-MIT Outing Club (rock climbing, winter skiing), and we were both in crew (she was cox and I was one of the rowers). I took ski lessons and wondered, in a letter to Mom:

> *I'm at the brink of a christy (doing traverses, stem turns, sideslipping). What is it I like about skiing? The muscle control? The windburn. The clumping around in heavy boots like a man? The grace and speed I am working towards?*

Competition turned me off: I loved fencing, except when our team competed with other colleges. I was in the Debate Club, but we debated Yale once and got trounced, so I didn't continue.

I MAJORED IN ENGLISH LITERATURE, which didn't include much creative writing. But I did take one class in essay-writing. My professor, Eleanor Prentiss would have us over for tea and we'd read Charles Lamb essays together. We'd learn that something can be spun out of anything and savor the words as delicious as the goodies she served us. Miss Prentiss thought that one of my essays was so good that I should submit it to a literary publication. It was a meditation on hedges. I didn't submit it—or even keep it—and I wonder now why I rejected my professor's faith in my potential.

I toyed with switching my major to geology. Ever since I hiked in the Sierras, which are made of granite, I loved rocks—but the male professor said that most geology jobs were in mining and I wouldn't be hired because women were considered "bad luck." I also considered majoring in sociology, where the teacher in one of my classes had us analyze issues of race and class. Miss Sussman suggested that I go South to support the growing civil rights movement, but her suggestion wasn't enough to move me to do so.

In the end, I stuck with English literature. For my "generals" (final paper that is in lieu of exams) I asked to write about Edna St. Vincent Millay, who was one of my favorite poets at the time: she wrote with a certain freedom about sexuality, held progressive political beliefs, and was fun to read. But my request was rejected and I was told that Millay was only "a minor writer," despite having won the Pulitzer Prize in 1923.

I think that by the 1950s, Millay was no longer considered "cool" and it was the modern male authors that were deemed to be esoteric and intellectual. So in the end I wrote on three male authors: Elizabethan dramatist John Webster, William Faulkner, and William Blake. Only Blake ("All the world in a grain of sand") had any personal meaning to me—his writing stayed with me while the others left no impression. But I'm confident that if I had been allowed to write about Millay, I would have found a way to make my paper interesting and it would have had great meaning to me. I wish I had fought more for her.

I now think that my decision to focus so exclusively on English was a mistake (I had even asked for, and received, the Dean's permission to take more than the expected number of credits in my major). Years later, I learned that Wellesley had great botany and economics departments, for instance, but I took no courses in either of them. There were so many subjects that I could have absorbed in those four years—when my mind was like a sponge, sucking up information and perspectives that would have helped me understand important aspects of the world for the rest of my life.

Extra-Curriculars

While at Wellesley, I attended "mixers," where guys from Boston-area colleges would dance just long enough to get your telephone number. They would then move on while you tried to memorize their names and faces so when they called you'd know which ones you wanted to date—or not. I dated an older medical resident from South Asia who took me to Indian cultural gatherings. I also dated two Harvard students, and "boys" from other area colleges.

All of those relationships were short-lived until my sophomore year, when I wrote to my mother that I'd met "John [sic] Beckwith." I told her that he had impressed me, in part, because while driving, he hummed to a Bach piece on the radio, then switched and hummed the "ground bass" part, which I'd just learned about in Music History 101. He soon had me interested in French philosophers and Russian novelists, and I got him reading poetry for the first time. We found that we shared an interest in Existentialism: a philosophy that declares that human life has no "given by God" meaning, so that each person must make their own meaning and decide how to live in this world. We went to movies, jazz clubs, poetry readings, and plays. After seeing Eugene O'Neil's *Long Days Journey into Night*, we had our first argument: I wanted to discuss the play immediately; Jon wanted to wait until it had "sunk in." Once we made up, our friendship (still platonic) was cemented.

By March, my argument was now with my parents. I wanted to visit Washington D.C. to see the sights and visit the museums. I argued to my parents that I needed to "discuss—not just contemplate—the sights" and so I needed Jon with me on the trip. My father would have taken the more stern approach, likely telling me something along the lines of: "You want to take a trip with this guy that you just met? What are you thinking?" It was probably my mother who persuaded him to let me go (she may have argued that "Barbara has common sense."). We did end up making the trip, staying—of course—in separate bedrooms, and taking in all that D.C. had to offer. I wrote a postcard home: "I am getting a big patriotic thrill out of Abe and Tom and George."

. . .

Each summer, I was expected to "broaden my horizons." In 1957, I spent the summer in Italy. Under the auspices of the Experiment in International Living, I traveled with a group of young people across the Atlantic. I taught Italian and dancing to other "experimenters" on the ship, writing home that "I have a bad accent and a very small vocabulary but I'm the only Italian teacher who has 100% attendance and new students every day." I lived for a month with the Bassano family (in Turin) and then traveled around Italy by bus with my group. Jon biked through Europe that same summer and came to see me in Turin, but we didn't relate well and I kind of snubbed him.

Before it was time to leave, I wrote to my parents to ask if I could stay in Italy (as two other students I knew were doing) to study for a year at the University of Florence, which would mean taking a leave of absence from Wellesley. I was in love with languages and attracted by the idea of the adventure of it all. My parents rejected my request. My mother shared her experience taking a similar risk: she'd gone to an international summer program but couldn't understand the lectures, despite having studied the language. Wellesley also said that I wouldn't get credits for courses I would take there, so staying in Italy was off the table. I came back from my summer trip visibly plump from the daily pasta, but dieted to get back in shape and held on to the Italian language, which helped when Jon and I later lived in Naples.

In the summer of 1958, I spent a month and a half at Oxford University (St. Hilda's College), studying Literature and Politics and the Arts of seventeenth century England, with a special seminar on Milton. Milton bored me, especially because his renowned poetry was so focused on religion. I lived in a one room flat and found myself in a mutual crush with a Greek student: Chrysostomos Savides. He wasn't fluent in English, so I probably felt powerful around him. He loved to play with language and we both loved poetry. I even thought about marrying him, or at least going to Greece to be near him.

I wrote to my mother: “Chrysostomos wants me to teach at Anatolia College. I want very much to start earning my own money and stop mooching (vulgar word but it’s emphatic) off my family.” Having a job was a major concern. Mom didn't argue with me; she just said “finish college first,” which I did. And then she suddenly decided she wanted to “visit me” (probably to check out Chrysostomos). She and I traveled around England, Scotland, and especially Wales, where we made a pilgrimage to poet Dylan Thomas’s home town and saw his *Under Milk Wood* at the annual festival in his honor.

I enjoyed the weeks I spent with my literature-loving mother in the U.K. She called the time “soul satisfying.” After she left, I wrote back to her:

> *I hope you’ve arrived home and still gay and extroverted. I found a wonderful avant-guard bookstore with the angry young man and beat generation—Henry Miller, Berthold Brecht, Samuel Beckett. And Ionesco and T. S. Eliot. I bought another Golding book—that bookstore was tempting.*

She wrote back: “I think I know why traveling is so wonderful—we see with the bright eager curiosity of children.”

She also wrote a postcard to my sister Joanne (from either Oxford or Cambridge), which provides visuals for what it was like to travel with my mother:

> *We just came back from a wild hour of punting (push a boat with a long pole) on this river. It is calm, narrow, winding, over-hung with bending trees, goes under numerous bridges—in short, very peaceful. But we started out in a drizzle and turned back in a downpour. It was very funny—we had rain-coats and an umbrella, but got soaked while all three poled, paddled, and steered back.*
>
> *I’m drying by a heater.*
>
> *- Love, Mom*

That summer I also took the biggest solo adventure of my life: I traveled around Europe, biking in the Loire area (chateaux of Villandry, Longeais) taking the train to France and Switzerland (Annecy, Chamonix; hiked in the Alps area), Germany (Strassburg, where I sketched Duhrer's art, then Munich), and then to Brussels where I went to the World's Fair. It was on this trip that I was able to fully experience art and culture on my own, free of the judgments of professors or guides. And it was on this trip that I got an appetite for bicycling. In one letter home I wrote:

> *There's something very satisfying about having each kilometer roll out from under you, each hill be felt as a line of sweat, each change in weather affecting you.*

Back at Wellesley, I audited Greek classes at Wellesley and wrote to Chrysostomos, but my interest in him faded (as my mother guessed it would). After a few weeks of Jon and I being "just friends," we got together romantically. I wrote home that while Chrysostomos was too much like me, Jon was more interesting because he was different.

Where's the Humor In It?

At my graduation ceremony in 1959, the commencement speaker, Secretary of Defense Neil McElroy, epitomized the era's feeling of the role of women: he spoke about the role of educated women, saying it was to *raise* (not *be*) the next generation of scientists, scholars and politicians. Former Secretary of State Madeleine Albright (my classmate) quoted him in her autobiography as saying:

> *"Your education here at Wellesley in the liberal arts tradition has given you an ideal preparation to serve as the very heart of a home, for the betterment of your family and your commu-*

nity...you have a duty to foster and multiply the society of educated men and women. This you can do most effectively in your own home, where education really starts."

As soon as I graduated, I wanted to "get away" for the summer—to study art. I went to Boulder, Colorado, where my cousin Betsey and her husband Royal Hassrick lived (both were artists). I rented a room in a suburban family's house (it came with a hotplate for making meals), with rent and expenses being paid for by my parents. I started to take drawing classes. The professor praised my work, but my art materials cost so much that I worked as an "on-call waitress" for banquets to pay for them. I wrote to Jon that "I dropped only one serving of chicken tonight and recovered it with great dignity."

Jon and I were both constantly reading at the time. I wrote a very opinionated letter to him, in which I argued:

I think you're attaching adjectives arbitrarily to E. Welty's work. Where is the evil in Death of a Traveling Salesman? And where is the humor in it? I don't have a copy of Curtain of Green though I have read from it. You make me want to read Proust. I can't stand Grandissime.

I read a Kafka-like story by Melville: Bartleby. I want now to read Pierre—have you heard of it? Kerouac mentions it as a bo-ho type thing in the Subterraneans, which I sympathize with up to page 30.

I am reading a polished, typical James Washington Square which is so well done it takes me away from the more "disturbing" books I have started.

Teaching & Travel

I spent the next year (1959-1960) getting my Master's in

Education from Tufts University in Medford, Massachusetts. I rented a one-room apartment (again with a hotplate) at 56 Boylston Street in Cambridge (renamed JFK Street in the 1980s). My landlady and another renter and I all shared a common bathroom. My grandfather's education fund was still supporting me, but not quite enough, so I supplemented by working briefly at the Mandrake Bookstore, where I was flummoxed by not knowing the answer when customers asked if we carried a particular book. After I fell down the steep stairs to the basement where books were stored, the owner, concerned about liability, fired me.

I then got a job as a waitress at Cronin's in Harvard Square (where Holyoke Center is now). This was the main college hangout at the time and we offered a 99-cent special of steak, potatoes, veggies, brownie, ice cream, and coffee. I remember being deeply bored each afternoon, waiting for the customers to come, and then when they did come, I'd be frantic at having to handle so many orders—the cook would yell at me sometimes and I'd cry. But the crowd was made up of students, including Jon and his friends, so it was still a "cool" place to work.

As part of my master's degree, I started student teaching at Cambridge High and Latin School, but was horrified by the English teacher who required students to stand and recite grammar rules word-for-word, with points off if you spoke an incomplete sentence—and no discussion at all. So I switched to Newton High School, probably with the help of Jon's dad, who chaired the Newton School Committee. But I alienated my "master teacher": she said that I'd disagreed with her in front of the students. The disagreement was something about Thomas Hardy's novels; I probably thought hearing different views would be stimulating for the students. So I switched again, to Meadowbrook Junior High School where I worked with an imaginative and supportive teacher. We took the students to Boston to see Shakespeare and I helped them run a school newspaper. My diary talks about offering my students help as they prepared to do a Shakespeare play, and to get rid of their Boston accents (my mother had worked hard to rid me of my New York/New Jersey accent, which I later wished I'd kept).

Making it Official

By 1960, Jon and I had been together for three years. We were skeptical of the convention of marriage, especially since my parents had divorced. I wrote to my younger sister Joanne:

> *When I see other young married couples, I get scared by the idea. Something to do with the publicness of being married. When you're unmarried, you can do things alone. You can meet other boys, you can quarrel when you want to, you can stand up for your own opinions, you can be selfish.*
>
> *Somehow I feel that when I am married, people will think they have a right to judge my conduct, my relationship to my husband, my happiness. I want to be my own version of a wife —not everybody else's.*

But a choice needed to be made: Jon was going to work in a microbiology lab in Berkeley, California, and I had found a teaching job there. We both thought that my teaching job would be in danger if they found out we were unmarried and living together. So we "gave in" and decided to get married. Jon first needed to finish his PhD at the University of Illinois at Champagne-Urbana, so I went out to Berkeley on my own and found a $90/month furnished apartment at 1433a Oxford Street, from which we could see the Bay when the fog lifted.

The job I found was at Burbank Junior High School, in the center of Berkeley, where the pay was $4,780 a year. I wrote my mother a letter which reveals that I went into teaching at this school with low expectations of my students of color:

> *I don't know how demanding or old-fashioned they will be about grammar and reading the classics. Perhaps the 60% Negro statistic suggests that they won't be pushing for arbitrary standards. Maybe it will mean having discipline and interest problems. Maybe both of these assumptions are prejudices.*

I am still haunted, wondering if my racist suppositions undermined my students' learning. I kept writings from the students from that year and they do show that I gave them some creative and challenging assignments.

Burbank was also clearly under-resourced: I had 170 students, and taught a range of ability levels. Like many first-time teachers, I had a hard time keeping "control" of my classroom. But the kids apparently liked me well enough: one student invited me to a family wedding reception, the first event in my life to that point where I was the only white person. But in the classroom, I would get confused when the Black kids would taunt each other, such as by saying "you have nappy hair!" I had no idea how to respond.

My first months of teaching and living alone made me so anxious that I lost a lot of weight and when I went back to get married in the gown that I'd been fitted for before leaving for California, I had to stuff kleenex into the bosom to fill it out.

In December, Jon and I returned to the East Coast to get married. The ceremony was in our family's Henryville house and Jon's friend Evan Geilich whisked me off in a car just before the ceremony's start-time, pretending, as a joke, to kidnap me. After the wedding, we had to leave the rest of the wedding party (they stayed through the weekend) to drive across the country so that I could resume teaching. We spent our first "honeymoon" night at a cheap hotel that advertised an erotic mattress, which (after we put coins in) bounced up and down so vigorously that we had to get off of it and wait for the ride to come to a halt.

~

Our bus leaving Fisk University when our exchange program ended

1955, "hanging out" at 210 Tower East, my dorm at Wellesley

4
BRASS RUBBINGS & RUE RABELAIS

Princeton

We had expected to stay in Berkeley, where I would teach at the junior high and Jon would do his post-doc work at Art Pardee's lab. But our plans changed when I got pregnant a few months later and, at the same time, Pardee moved his lab to Princeton University. We would now be moving to Princeton, New Jersey. The result was that I left my first teaching job after one year, adding to the stereotype of women teachers at the time, that they'd "abandon teaching for motherhood," (implying that "spinster" teachers were more reliable).

We drove back across the country with detours to national parks along the way, including Mt. Lassen, Crater Lake, Mt. Rainier, Glacier National Park, the Grand Tetons, and the Black Hills. We learned to not camp by rivers (the mosquito hangout spot) and had our first campground encounters with bears (who ate our food) and skunks (who invaded our tent).

In 1961, Jon and I found an inexpensive apartment on Bank Street in Princeton, where we had to contend with cockroaches and mice, so we soon moved to junior faculty apartments. I met Gail and Michael Graves, who were also living there, and I am still friends with Gail today, 64 years later. I was able to find a part-time job correcting papers for English teachers at the high school, which I could do at home. Ben was born soon after, at Princeton Hospital.

I did a lot of reading that year. My college courses had fed my love of literature and now that I was liberated from reading "for an assignment," I could instead explore a wider range of authors. It helped that Jon and my woman friend Haralyn Dubin joined me: we wanted to talk about books and the ideas they explored—it's what we did for fun. The authors we focused on were struggling with grand ideas and came from a variety of backgrounds, like French novelist André Malraux, Russian author Leo Tolstoy, Edith Wharton, Willa Cather (who wrote about life on the Great Plains), J.D. Salinger, American novelist Bernard Malamud, French author André Gide, Harlem Renaissance author Ralph Ellison, Italian novelist and poet Cesare Pavese, and Italian Holocaust survivor Primo Levi.

That was also the year of the Cuban Missile Crisis, when Americans were convinced that President Kennedy was going to drop atomic bombs on Cuba and start a nuclear war that would kill us all. For the first time in my life, I was sure that I was about to die. Fortunately, Russia "blinked."

"The Isles"

AFTER PRINCETON, Jon's scientific pursuits transported us to England, where we lived in London and Cambridge, and then Paris. In London, we rented an apartment in what had previously been a mansion on Lancaster Gate, but had been carved up into separate apartments. It was grand (bedrooms, kitchenette and bathroom converted from what had been a large ballroom), with oversized mirrors and floor to ceiling windows overlooking Kensington Gardens. Ben and I regularly went to the Gardens and to a rarely-visited "nature park" where I let him run naked.

I was content, more or less, with being a mother (I had time to make all of my dresses by hand), but the idea of having a job still pulled at me. While Ben attended nursery schools in London, I searched for a job teaching English to non-native speakers—but I couldn't find any. I almost signed up to be a model at art classes: until I discovered that those ads were fronts for prostitutes.

Ben would turn two years old in December of 1963. A month before his birthday, President John F. Kennedy was assassinated in Dallas, Texas, which was front page news overseas. Jon paced back and forth, not knowing how to process the news. I wrote in my journal that Benjamin was upset that Jon was upset. I didn't write about my own response at the time: my "job" as a mother outweighed my concern as an American citizen living abroad.

We traveled a bit to the southwestern coast of England, including Cornwall. When Dad came to visit, he and Ben and I drove to Chester, and then to Scotland, staying in hotels and at least one night in a bread and breakfast, which Dad loved because he so enjoyed talking to people.

We moved again in 1964, when Jon's job took him to Cambridge, England, where he worked in Sydney Brenner's lab. We lived at 56 Glisson Road, a brick row house with a walled-in back yard, snails clinging to the damp brick wall. The house was wet and chilly, with the only warmth coming from portable heaters: Jon would hold off using the bathroom until he got to work. Ben went to a wonderful nursery school run by a rich American woman named Rothchild.

I ALWAYS SEEM to need a project: in England, it was brass rubbings. I'd drive to a church, get down on my hands and knees, and make a paper rubbing of the long brass images of families buried in the cemetery, including at Westley Waterless, St. Breoch, Isleham, St. Columb/John Arundel, Queen's Chapel, Christi Chapel, Little

Sheltford, 14 and 15th century Hinxton, and Hildersham. I still have the rubbings stored in our attic, rolled up like parchments.

We also traveled to Germany and Holland (Jon had a conference in Schevenignen), where we did some easy bicycling on flat roads. We traveled to Greece in our Deux Cheveaux *traction avant* (we called it the "gangster car"), where we got lost on mountain roads. We were invited into a family's home where, not knowing English, they struggled using hand motions to tell us the news that Neil Armstrong had just walked on the moon.

We took a trip to Morocco for 10 days in 1964 (I was very pregnant with Anthony) leaving Ben and his new friend Johnny Hershey with an English farm family. We passed briefly through Spain on the way to Morocco, Franco's scary machine-gun wielding soldiers standing at all state buildings—including museums—in Madrid. When we arrived in northern Africa, I was struck by the many young children working alongside their parents; the "scribes" in plazas, writing letters for illiterate people; and how I couldn't talk with women because most were covered and didn't even look at me. I also started to get upset at being away from Ben for so long. Ben may have been upset too, because he later wrote in an elementary school assignment that we'd left him on a farm for "two years."

We expected that travel after Anthony was born would be more difficult, so the three of us took a "last trip" to England's rocky Cornish coast. In a postcard to my mother, I wrote that "Benjamin goes with us on our walks and has good stamina. He enjoys whatever we do."

We were back in Cambridge by July and I was nine months pregnant. The English health authorities didn't allow me to have Anthony at a hospital because my first birth had been uneventful. Most non-hospital births took place at home back then, but I was allowed, as an American, to have Anthony in a kind of nursing home.

I'd been required to take natural childbirth classes (Jon was not invited) which meant that I wasn't knocked out during birth. The doctor never even arrived—the nurse tried to finish her tea, but Anthony came so fast that she and I delivered him on our own. Natural childbirth helped me later in life: when I was hiking, rock climbing, biking or running 10K races, I knew how to let my lower body accept whatever it had to go through, while my upper body could disengage and stay relaxed. My friend Barbara Signer brought me champagne and strawberries the next day, which a hospital would not have allowed.

Paris

It was in Paris that Jon's dream to work with François Jacob and Jacques Monod came true when he was accepted to the Pasteur Institute. While living in Paris, we took trips (with both kids) to Lake Como in Switzerland, Poitou and Anjou in France, and the island of Sicily. Traveling was decidedly more difficult with children, but it seemed like the Italians talked with us *because* of our two kids: the women would tell me Ben was too skinny and that we needed to fatten him up.

We lived in Paris for a year, renting a furnished house on Rue Rabelais in Vanves, just outside of Paris. The sculptor Krishna Reddy lived in the same complex, as did another ceramics artist (a piece of Reddy's art was installed in a German bank, but it exploded, as ceramics sometimes do). Our neighbor, Michelle Boulesteix, who had a son a bit older than Ben, occasionally babysat. Ben went to a Montessori nursery school run by nuns for a while and I took French classes at the Alliance Francaise. To practice my understanding, I read plays by Moliere, looking up the words I didn't know, and then went to performances of those plays. At home, Ben soon spoke a blend of English and French: "I want to mange" (eat) and "That boy's sauteing." (jumping).

WE MOVED BACK to the United States in 1965. Jon joined the Harvard Medical School faculty and was to run his own microbiology lab. I don't remember how I felt about coming "home," but after awhile I did feel nostalgia for the excitement and the challenges that came with living abroad, always wondering: where are we going next?

We first rented a small Cambridge apartment in a large building at 992 Memorial Drive, directly across from the Charles River. I remember the refreshing breeze and the great view. There was just one other couple with kids in the building, but when our families joined a babysitting pool, Ben and Anthony met other kids, including Patrick and Matthew Barton.

Two years later, in 1967, after the Bartons had moved to Appleton Street, we learned that the second floor apartment next door to them, at 8A Appleton Road, was available. We rented the apartment from Stanley Chao for $200 a month. Two years later, we bought the two-family home for $42,000. We had always wanted to raise our children in the city: in addition to our mostly positive experiences in Berkeley, Princeton, London, Cambridge, and Paris, we were also rejecting our own suburban upbringings —and I've always associated the suburban lifestyle with my mother's drinking and with her isolation from work opportunities. The funny thing is, I also remember thinking at the time that our move from Memorial Drive (just three blocks from Harvard Square) to Appleton Road felt like we were moving "way out there"—almost like moving to the suburbs—even though it was only a few blocks away.

Activism and Community Involvement

In the late 1960s into the early 1970s, I threw myself into the school and city affairs of Cambridge—a role young parents often take on, especially those who are not working. For a time, I was the president of Tobin School Parent Teachers Association, but I later wondered why I didn't step back from that position and ask active Black parents Faith and Ed Chase to lead—or did they want me to do it?

I was also the president of the Cambridge Council of PTAs and joined the Cambridge Civic Association (CCA). I immersed myself in Cambridge civic life: as Clerk and School Affairs Chair of the CCA, I did research, developed policies and platforms, wrote articles, edited the newsletter, and worked for candidates. I worked for various school committee candidates. Active women like myself were asked to run for office. But I didn't think that I was up to that kind of challenge: I was mostly nervous about the expectation that I would be able to spout off figures and statistics when asked about them, as politicians seemed to do with such ease.

As a member of Cambridge's Civic Unity Committee and head of its Education Committee, I worked to get Black teachers and more diverse curriculum into the schools at all levels. For the committee, I compiled and distributed to high schools a list of books by African-Americans, for potential use in their libraries or in English classes. Our committee also interviewed candidates for Superintendent of Schools and recommended Alflorence ("Al") Cheatham, who became Cambridge's first Black school superintendent. He accomplished a lot, but he ended up resigning after three years, citing an ulcer from "the pressures of work." Were the racial tensions in the city at the time part of what contributed to his leaving? I suspect they were, but it's hard to know for sure.

I worked with others to win community support and city council funding for a new Community Schools program, which is now active in every neighborhood in the city. It was a way to use school buildings for afterschool programs for children and adults; we hired the first coordinators for that program. I also worked with Katya Peters to launch Cambridge School Volunteers and an enrichment program that made Children's Museum kits available for schools and classroom aides. Katya and I went around and delivered the kits to different schools around the city. We also set up a speakers program to be available to every teacher in the system.

I wanted so much to be a working person that I also took part-time jobs, including jobs as a "theme reader" for high school teachers in Belmont (1965-1966), Woburn (1969-1970) and Cambridge High and Latin and Cambridge Rindge Technical School (1971). The job of a theme reader was to evaluate students' written work and hold individual conferences with them, along with making writing sequence suggestions to teachers. I also found a jobs as a tutor for an Italian boy, as a volunteer tutor for non-English-speaking students, and as a social studies aide.

I was increasingly thinking about the fact that my part-time and volunteer jobs were optional for me—Jon's salary supported the family— and that our family did not need my paltry pay. This awareness found its way into my writing, as can be seen in a poem I wrote about a woman worker at a small café: each morning before work, Jon and I would walk or bike to Harvard Square for coffee and croissants at the Patisserie Française, a small basement-level bakery on Boylston Street, with a few chairs and tables outside on the tiny brick landing. I eventually got to know the woman who served us each morning and came to realize something about her—she was a woman who worked "to survive":

You serve me coffee every day
stand for hours behind the counter
people are rude or polite to you
in no dependable order
You listen to me
I listen to you
in between customers
and cleaning off the tables

Your talk is hard as nails
You've been burned before
by your boss, by men
You hate rich people
and women who hang on men
Your son comes for coffee
You wait on him
You were going to school to get out of this dead-end job
Then your house burns down
Your son knocks up a girl
You take them both in, quit school, and work overtime
We talk between customers about our sons and our wishes
I know your excellence, you know mine
We are strangers, we are sisters.

On April 4, 1968, Dr. Martin Luther King Jr. was assassinated in Memphis, Tennessee, followed by Bobby Kennedy on June 6, in Los Angeles. There was despair, anger, and civil unrest in Boston. Jon and I supported the Black Panther free health care clinic (Jon gave his Eli Lilly award money to that Boston program and to the defense fund for the Panther 13, jailed on conspiracy charges that a judge later dismissed). We were aware of the racial tensions, but, sadly, my main takeaway from the unrest that followed was that I felt I wouldn't be welcome anymore in Roxbury, where we used to go to bookstores and other shops. While communities of color coped with discrimination in every institution, our financially stable lives would continue without trauma. We could easily escape job or other stresses via travel and nature.

We had decided not to buy or rent a "summer home" like so many financially comfortable people did. Instead, we would travel each summer. Our decision was influenced, I think, by the Beckwiths' Lake Wakeby summer place on the Cape, which was beautiful but which Jon saw as more of a burden: "cut the grass, Jonny, wash the dishes," he recalls his mother repeatedly telling him.

With the kids, we drove across the country twice over the coming years, both times to be part of Sierra Club mountain backpacking trips. Ben took to them more than Anthony, who didn't get excited about hiking until decades later. We took notes on everything we experienced. One note read: "Ben spotted a gopher coming out of one of his many holes and cutting down one leaf, then another, then a whole plant, dragging them back into his hole. Two feet away. He wasn't afraid of us." We also visited friends in Hershey, Pennsylvania, drove to Cape Breton Island where we camped for a month in a big tent, and camped in the White Mountains, where we delighted in feeling the Swift River carry us down its whitewater chute.

In 1969, I worked as a Boston Public Schools English as a Second Language teacher in the federal WIN program for Spanish-speaking adults and then at a school in Uphams Corner in the Dorchester neighborhood of Boston. The program was new and the textbooks so inadequate that I created my own curriculum and effective methods of teaching.

I enjoyed the students (knowing some Spanish certainly helped) and they enjoyed me; they even invited me home for dinner. But I quit the job when I saw how the administrators treated people: someone had complained about the program and their solution was to bring the students to a room and sit and grill them about who complained—it felt very disrespectful. Looking back, I regret that I didn't stay and insist on change.

~

In this idealistic era (late 1960s/early 1970s), we decided that we wanted to live semi-communally with our friends Dan and Phyllis Connell and their kids. As part of the plan, we informed our tenants Junie Patt and Leah Sibley (sisters, both in their 70s), that they would have to leave the downstairs apartment to make room for the Connells. To this day, I've felt remorse at how indifferent we were to how this would impact and even traumatize them, so intent were we on our utopian communal living idea. Fortunately, both for my conscience and for Junie and Leah, our experiment ended before it started when the Connells told us that they were breaking up.

In addition to the Connells, we were making friends with interesting people all around Cambridge and the Boston area. I have a record of what the "scene" was like because when I taught high school, I gave an assignment to my students: "*The Culture of my friends: analyze your own group's values and shared assumptions and habits*"—as part of the process, I also completed the assignment, describing our 1970s friends' culture:

> *We meet to eat together, dance, drink, go to movies, do things outdoors, meet at gathering spots like T.T. the Bears and the Women's Restaurant. We drop in to each other's houses unannounced. We talk about left politics, a movie, interactions between people and our own personal problems. We check each other out for how we are doing with the people we are living with.*
>
> *When we get in a good mood, we laugh a lot. It seems to be an unwritten understanding that we won't tease each other but instead will be open and honest if there is something or someone is doing that we don't like. We share our deepest problems easily. We don't brag or compete with each other. We value adventure and like to try things we have never done before. We all love foreign foods because we are well-traveled.*

We don't "talk shop" if there are people present who don't do the same job.

We spend a lot of time trying to figure out why we and other people feel and act as they do. We all believe in equal sex roles and equal work roles, so we all bring food when we eat together so no one will slave for the rest of us. We don't let anyone dominate the conversation or interrupt other people.

We don't use swear words that refer to sex because we all think they are sexist. We believe in being healthy, exercising, not smoking. We share the use of our car, groceries, records, books, camping equipment, dance tapes, clothes. We feel comfortable sleeping over at anyone's house after a party, etc. We all have casual, not very neat houses, with inexpensive possessions.

We treat teenagers in our midst with respect, or at least we believe in doing so. We value seeing each other in different combinations, not always as one group, and we don't get upset if two or three of us want to do something without the rest. We feel free to hug each other and tell each other what we like about each other.

We all believe in working on and working out problems: we all accept that there will always be a lot of problems needing working out.

The 1960s and 70s were a time to break with both the laws and the norms of the 1950s. We smoked marijuana, but never tried anything else. I considered taking LSD, but felt I would be too vulnerable to its distortions. We'd go to nude beaches with the kids. We were offered cocaine once at a party, but weren't interested. We considered ourselves generic "socialists." I took a course in Marx, but found it boring. We were both heavily involved in the group Science for the People, where our meetings included "criticism/self-criticism."

Political movements sometimes vied with each other, each claiming "political correctness" that the right wing later used against leftists. Some academics quit and went to work in factories and organize "the people." I was skeptical—and as usual, full of questions:

Come down, Marx
Is there hope?
Are people smart?
Do co-ops help?
Should we vote a leader?
Can we work with racists?
Are there too many people?
Should women work alone?
Should we ally on this issue?
Come down, Marx
I need answers to questions of my own

THE 1970S WAS ALSO the era of the Women's Liberation movement, which opened up new ways of thinking about the roles women play in family, work, and community. "Women's Lib" transformed lives, including mine. One 1978 book—*A History of Women in America,* by Carol Hymowitz and Michaele Weissman—led me to a realization: we ordinary women were part of history and our stories deserved to be known. I agreed:

> *I never did like history: so much to memorize, everything lined up, sewed up, nothing to wonder about, to imagine. So I go for what's too minor to care about, what has no history. I go for the holes. Including the chasm of women's lives.*

I still remember the moment at a party when, while talking to a group of women, I realized that they were just as "valuable" to talk to as men. I joined a consciousness-raising group and confronted Jon about what I considered his domination in our relationship. We had lots of arguments about what words to use to refer to women ("woman" rather than "girl", "Ms." rather than "Mrs." or "Miss"). I deliberately threw away my wedding ring in opposition to the cultural requirement for women to show that they are either married or "still available." I cut my long red hair and stopped wearing makeup. I snapped back at men when they harassed me on my 6.2 mile runs around Cambridge, or when the hardware store owner demanded that I smile before giving me change. A group of us leafleted the Playboy Club in Boston to protest the "bunny" outfits women were required to wear. We put "This ad insults women" stickers on sexist posters and pages of magazines.

Years before I became involved in activism, my sister Linda had put her body on the line for her beliefs. In August of 1960, she and her husband Peter were part of a Quaker group that joined the Committee for Non-Violent Action for a week-long 135-mile walk from Boston to New London, Connecticut. They were marching to oppose the increasing proliferation of nuclear warheads (in particular to protest the construction of Polaris Submarines in New London). They pushed a stroller carrying their toddler Jennifer, staying at pre-arranged homes along the way for the grueling week of travel by foot. Upon reaching New London, there were days of meetings and civil disobedience actions, leading to some arrests. And when Harvard Square's Woolworths was being picketed in support of lunch counter sit-ins in the South, I refrained from shopping there, but Peter and Linda showed up to protest. Linda was told she was too pregnant to be on a picket line, but Peter stayed and went directly to the store's Boston headquarters to press higher-ups to do what was right. Only later did I become aware that they had opposed the same kind of armaments that I later opposed.

Jon and I and the kids continued to travel, including driving to Quebec, New Brunswick, and Montreal in 1970 on a camping trip. Our first night of the trip was in Vermont and we got flooded out of our family-sized tent. We realized too late that we were supposed to treat our tent with waterproofing.

Back home, I led a Great Books discussion group at the Belmont Public Library, following the lead of my mother, who participated in Great Books discussions for years. I had been intrigued by Mom's group, made up of suburbanites who wanted to grapple with big ideas and find the meaning for themselves in the books they read. In our group, we read and discussed classical writings in philosophy, political theory, and literature. The core Great Books discussion technique that stuck with me, one that would always stimulate deep conversation, was to ask "why" questions for which *I* had no answers.

When Jon took a six month sabbatical in Naples, Italy, in 1971, my work was again shown to be secondary: the whole family moved to Naples for six months. I did find work there as a substitute teacher for a few days at the John F. Kennedy School of Naples, where our boys went to school. I remember doing all kinds of imaginative things with the kids (for example, studying the lizards that ran around outside the school as a way to counteract the kids' game of pulling their tails off). I also organized the library for the K-12 school.

We lived in a furnished professor's apartment (with a grand piano) in Posillipo, one of Naples' loveliest hill neighborhoods. I loved speaking Italian—it was such an expressive language—and the food was delicious. I tried to explore the city, but at that time any woman walking outside without an older woman as chaperone was considered "loose" (if not a prostitute—at least one man approached me assuming that of me). As a man, Jon did not have this kind of negative experience, but it certainly colored my view on Italian men.

To appear as a respectable professional, I'd take a bus, with notebook in hand, to the American Library, immersing myself in linguistics, which turned out to be great preparation for my later jobs as a teacher. Four months into the half-year sabbatical, Ben fell (or jumped) from a tree and broke his arm. We were warned that Neapolitan medical care wasn't good enough and Ben was in constant pain, so he and I flew back to Boston. The doctors there were horrified at the tight cast they'd put on Ben in Italy and even told us not to return.

Back In the U.S.

BEN AND ANTHONY were soon busy with school and with their groups of friends. Ben had a newspaper delivery job, getting up at 5:30 a.m (Anthony got the same job a few years later). I had no job, but was active as a volunteer in communal projects, like the local baby-sitting pool and the Fresh Pond Food Co-op. For the co-op, I would drive to the sprawling Chelsea distribution center to pick up the boxes of pre-ordered food to bring back to my neighbors.

I was becoming more political. I did "court watching" for the American Friends Service Committee program and for the Black Panthers on trial ("harassment arrests"), to lend my white skin's assumed credibility. I also went door-to-door to get support for rent control (which passed), to end the Vietnam War, and later to support United Farm Workers boycotts. This canvassing experience firmed up my anti-elitist values: I still remember my long talks about housing problems in apartment hallways, and listening to an elderly woman talking about the war for an hour while her two dogs barked at me incessantly.

Around this time, we drove with our kids and some friends to West Virginia to visit "Maggie's Farm," where we stayed for several days. Maggie lived in a crowded trailer with dogs and her boyfriend. She ground her own bread flour and made her own grapefruit wine; the kids remember the farm as "a commune." They were true hippies.

1970s Outdoors Adventures

A MONTH-LONG VACATION found us driving across the country (during a hot July) from Massachusetts, through New York, Pennsylvania, Ohio, Iowa, Nebraska, Arizona, Nevada, and Colorado. We wrote a family journal together and Ben, the future songwriter, turned our grueling car ride into a poem/song:

> *I've been in the car for about 12 hours, I've seen at least 13 radio towers. We've stopped at least 2 times to rest, out in the wilderness, out in the West.*

We went on a family Sierra Club Wilderness trip to the Emerald Lakes in the Sierras. We hiked with backpacks while horses carried our gear. We drove back across country, on a more northerly route. I loved feeling each mile of our vast country unroll beneath us while we absorbed the geography and culture of each state. I'll never forget the wonder I felt for the wildly varied land we covered.

We took a second family trip in 1974 to Colorado's San Juan Mountains. I got so mellow that I'd walk for hours without talking, just touching the flowers as I passed them. Our group was supposed to be picked up at the end by a train, but it was delayed by a forest fire. We could have been left stranded with not enough food, but we were able to get out and after this trip, felt confident enough to hike on our own (no more guide-led hiking or biking for us).

In February, we all visited Dad (and Disneyland and the Everglades) in Florida and then traveled to Puerto Rico, where we stayed in a small town resort and the kids swam all day long. Our attempt at snorkeling was short-lived: the sea urchins frequenting the bay scared us.

While the kids were at camp one summer, Jon and I hiked in the Cascades in Washington state and Garibaldi Lake in British Columbia. We drove to Vancouver and Tweedsmuir Provincial Park, where there were no trails: the ranger said we'd have to hike with two other couples because only one among us had detailed topographic maps. One couple we hiked with were from Chicago and they had their four-year-old daughter "Revi" with them. We learned that "Revi" was short for "Revolutionary Hope." The other couple, Tammy and Jim, became our good friends for years to come. We found that all three couples loved, and could quote from, feminist poet Marge Piercy—and two of them even brought the same book of hers on the trip. It was wild and wonderful, except for when Jon and I were making our way back to our campsite with no trail to guide us in dense fog. The fog cleared just in time for us to see that if we'd taken one more step, we would have fallen off a cliff.

Back in Cambridge, there were other adventures: my friends Steve Aldrich, Steve Bzomowski, Susan Michaels and I snuck into the old decrepit basement squash courts in Harvard's Adams House. We didn't quite understand squash yet, but had a great time trying to figure it out. I also had a "gang" of my own outdoor adventurers, which included Steve Burden, Steve Bzomowski, Gene Thompson, Judy Livingston, and a guy named Dean. We went whitewater canoeing on the Battenkill in Vermont, the Dead River, the Saco and the Androscoggin in Maine. We also went rock-climbing at the Quincy Quarries. Our climbing with ropes stopped when our friend Dean, who had been the ropes expert, mysteriously disappeared. We later learned that he had joined the CIA.

In 1976 and again in 1977, I went on winter camping adventures, one of which was a solo one-night outing in 20-degree weather, by snowshoe, on the New Hampshire property of Home Base School outdoors teacher Bert Hirtle. It was my way to "embrace" New England weather. I made mistakes, which I detailed in an article that three publications wanted because they showed so clearly what *not* to do.

~

Me, Ben, and Anthony, c.1969

5
FINDING A HOME BASE

I wanted so much to teach that in 1972 I did volunteer work for a year at both Cambridge's Pilot School (where I also sometimes subbed for pay) and at Group School, a Cambridge independent high school for low-income and working class youth. The Group School curriculum focused on positive class, gender, and ethnic identities. Being middle class, I may not have been the the teacher they needed, but I followed the lead of Larry Aronson and Phyllis Ewen. I wrote that:

> *I enjoy working in two schools this year: each gives me a perspective on the other. But I don't want to go without a paid job for more than one year, though I'm not sure how I'll get myself a job.*

In 1973, I moved on from volunteer work and was hired by the Pilot School, a Cambridge alternative public school program of 180 students who were chosen by lottery to represent a cross-section of the city racially, economically, academically, and by neighborhood. Pilot, housed on one floor of Rindge Tech, focused on close human relationships, individualized learning, and student decision-making. I co-taught or supervised several interns, volunteers and independent studies, and was advisor to the school newspaper (I got in trouble when kids wrote something that Principal Sweeny didn't like). I also was an advisor to 20 students.

I wrote to my father:

> *The greatest thing is to see a kid grow through the years. We emphasize trying college out more than we should, perhaps, but we encourage all kids to try every option. It's great to see a kid come from a Catholic elementary school, go wild with the relative freedom of Pilot, then get to know some upperclassmen and teachers, get involved in some good projects, and slowly start to discipline himself. Or to see a project kid come to the school sullen and end up playing a part in a play, or speaking up for student rights or taking on the editorship of the newspaper, or applying to really hard college, or doing a 50-hour solo in the White Mountains.*

I taught classes with students from all four grades and of all skill levels. I created courses like *Real People*—an interviewing course (music journalist Elijah Wald was one of my best students). Students would decide who to invite and would interview and write up their interviews. Invitees included a teacher who was adopted, a student who was dyslexic, another student who ran away from home, and an African American doctor. One of the interviewees was from a gay and lesbian group, which gave me a reputation as being gay-friendly (students like Jim Vetter and teachers like Arthur Lipkin saw me as an ally in making schools safe for gay members).

I devised a multi-cultural *Mythology* course (Norse, Greek, African, American Indian) and a *Children's Fantasies* course, where students studied child development and shared childhood memories. They evaluated books in terms of interest, sexism, and racism, they wrote children's books, and they did readings for kids in nursery schools in the city. For my *Cambridge City Govern-*

ment course, I drove students around their different neighborhoods and to the recycling center, and the police station—we also interviewed the mayor (Alfred Velluci). In my *Modern American Writers* course, we read Hemingway, Fitzgerald, Steinbeck, Wright, Baldwin, Angelou, Malamud, and Nabokov; the students ushered so they could see Kesey's "One Flew Over a Cuckoo's Nest" for free. We saw a free dress rehearsal of Tennessee Williams "A Streetcar Named Desire."

Producing a Newspaper was a course that didn't go so well. It was the Black Power era and a group of Black students in the class were blunt about saying: "I don't like you," and I had no idea how to deal with their anger. I did, however, give them an outlet for their ideas and activism. And I contributed my perspective with my usual frank realism and questions for which I had no answer:

> *We've named our newspaper Unity, an ideal that a lot of people at Pilot School have. But one of the problems I see is that the black kids are really getting together with each other, working on unifying together, and there is just so much hope, trust and caring that a person can give out, so they don't have much to spare on getting together with whites. And white kids aren't getting themselves together over anything in particular, because they don't feel oppressed as a group, and don't have any unifying energy that could go into unifying with black kids.*
>
> *The crafts group is mostly white. The wilderness program is mostly white. The cultural group is black. Sacramento Street parties are black. The Carnival was mostly black. We rub elbows, that's all.*
>
> *Are the needs and interests too different to justify Unity as a goal? Does the black unifying reduce the black/white unifying that could be going on? Would more black/white unity stop the black unity that's growing? How do you feel about it?*

The Pilot School faculty would hold meetings with discussions that seemed overly intellectual to me. But they seemed to think that I was wishy-washy: not standing up to the kids, listening too much to their side. They were probably right: I had too much of my mother ("Use your best judgment, dear") and not enough of my father ("This is what you have to do"). Meanwhile, the guidance counselor, when angered by student behavior, would simply announce she was quitting, a "control technique" I didn't agree with. I was, at this time, not confident in myself or my teaching skills, but I now wish that I'd aired my views to her.

Jon's activism in science drew him to involvement in the group *Science for the People* and in the late 1970s I began writing articles for their magazine and joined the editorial board. I edited and proofread articles, worked with writers to improve them, helped lay out pages for the magazine, and co-wrote several articles with Jon. At one point I wrote: "SFTP seems to be trying to 'clean up our own house' by examining how we dominate each other at our own meetings. It's very exciting."

It was around this time that I read Margaret Walker's 1966 novel *Jubilee* and it affected me deeply. Years later, I compiled a list of "Books that Matter to Me" and said this about *Jubilee*:

> *The book turned my stereotypes about the South upside down. Walker tells a saga as gripping as* Gone With the Wind, *but from Black characters' points of view. It was one of the first books that made me realize that what I read in history books and see in movies is not necessarily "the truth."*

When I was working at the schools, I grew concerned after seeing the Educational Development Corporation (EDC) curriculum that suggested that men and women's social roles were based in genetics. I joined Jon's Sociobiology study group (which welcomed nonscientists and the diverse perspectives they bring) and co-led a workshop critiquing sociobiology in high school textbooks at an American Biology Teachers Conference, and also at Harvard Epworth. Some of us met with EDC representatives to try to get biologically deterministic curricula changed.

Around this same time, I drafted an article that questioned the importance that teachers and parents would often put on I.Q. test results. I pointed out that their trust in that single-number measurement of intellectual worth was not based on real knowledge of what was in those tests. I found that some teachers appeared to put their students into two categories: "smart" or "not smart." For the article, I asked those teachers to name what *they* were "bad at" and whether anything in their upbringing may have led to that deficiency. In their responses, they would name an embarrassing incident or a carping teacher that had blocked them from pursuing a skill or an art. Oddly, the reason that I abandoned the article was that the head of the school, who had just completed her doctorate, told me I couldn't write such an article if I hadn't first done an academically rigorous "study." I was sure she was wrong, but I gave in to her view.

JON and I also went to Paris that year, staying with our French friends Maxime Schwartz and Brigitte Giquel in their apartment overlooking the vibrant market street, Rue Daguerre. We then drove west to Brittany, spending time in Brigitte's centuries-old family cottage in the hamlet of Jarnay, bicycling around the rural countryside.

When I was in my 40s, I enjoyed challenging myself physically. I started running a lot, inspired by the 10K women's races, which were sponsored by Bonnie Bell (a cosmetics company, of all things, that launched the races in reaction to men-only marathons).

At the time, I wrote:

There was a 5 mile race in June 10 that I signed up for called "Run for Women who Run for Office" whose proceeds go to different women running for political office (Mass Political Women's Caucus which endorses liberal women candidates). 600 women ran. I made the same time as my last run, darn it. I like to have my time creep down, even if it's just one minute each time I'm in a race.

I gave my students an assignment to write a "2-minute story" and I wrote my own sample story about what it's like to finish a race:

My breath rasped and my chest heaved painfully. My mouth was dry from being open and rushing through the air for so long. My hands flopped loosely at my side, but the rest of my body strained as far as my mind could make it. I was in the midst of a violent argument with myself. Half of my mind was on the verge of saying "What the hell, give up, it's not worth it."

But the other half was arguing, "Just think of it like the dentist—in a few moments it will all be over." And the mechanical part of my mind was simply calculating the risk of trying a final spurt and maybe collapsing as against continuing at a steady pace for the final few yards but being sure of finishing. Meanwhile, my nostrils breathed in acrid oil and gas fumes. My muscles struggled against the wind and the aching of my leg.

My ears throbbed with the dull roar inside my head. But the people, the people yelling wildly, clapping, admiring, cheering—the people drove me on. Passing the marker and the outstretched arms, I tried to stop my body, but it seemed to rush on, knocking me wildly into the runner before me, making me reach out to people to keep from falling.

Something metallic-tasting rose to my mouth. The heat in my cheeks changed to cool lines of sweat dripping down. I heard myself give a little cry with every breath. The people with their smiles and their stares as they wondered how it must be to be as tired as I looked, was sweet salve that made me grin through my salty sweat-tears.

After four or five years of running on Cambridge's concrete sidewalks, my back started acting up and I had to stop all exercises for a year or two. Around this time, I took a gymnastics class. I was at least a decade older than the other members of the class. I didn't pursue it further, though, because the instructor insisted that we end each move with graceful "female" poses, which I objected to. To be frank, I also couldn't lift my rear end up over the bar, a basic move in gymnastics.

My running would sometimes even find an intersection with racial justice activism. In 1979, I ran a race that went through Roxbury, to raise money for groups fighting violence against women and to protest a series of murders of Black women in the Boston area. In the course of five months, eleven Black women and one white woman were murdered in Roxbury and the crimes did not receive nearly enough attention from the media—it was left to Black feminist groups such as the Combahee River Collective to push for answers and police response.

In the winter, I led Gene and Steve and son my Ben on a winter camping trip to Newcomb Lake, deep in New York state's Adirondack Mountains. But it was a life-threatening 22 degrees below zero. We survived, and the experience led to the first of several of my "disaster story" essays, which readers loved: I realized that tales of my dangerous mistakes could amuse *and* warn others what not to do:

At our first water stop, we found our canteens had iced up—not just crusted, but frozen solid. We were forced to sucking moisture from the snow...

Four miles later, the daylight fading already, we realized we didn't know where we were...

We never did reach the campsite; we camped instead in a kind of dell where at least we'd be out of the gusting wind. Not until that moment had I considered the problem of how to stake down a tent in four feet of fluffy snow.

I needed mental challenges as well, so I signed up for adult education classes in photography (I took some nice outdoor black and white photos), car mechanics (all of which I forgot), and American History (this was the first time that I had seen a textbook —pre-Howard Zinn—that took a non-conventional approach to history, discussing issues of power, class, and race that my high school textbooks had left out or glossed over). The Cambridge Center for Adult Education is a treasure.

My mother had recently developed throat cancer, caused or exacerbated by smoking and drinking. For over two years, she suffered through chemotherapy and radiation treatments, but finally had to have her larynx removed. At this point, I was driving to Henryville often to see her. She tried hard to learn esophageal speech, "burping" up air to speak words. When she finally resorted to a mechanical voice box, she rose to the challenge and became adept at short, funny remarks.

Mom refused a second round of chemo. Determined to live her last year at home, she paid for round-the-clock nurses, but suffered increasing pain because they weren't allowed to give her adequate painkillers. At the time, addiction concerns trumped relief from pain, even in a terminal case.

In the early fall of 1978, I sat by mom's bed in Henryville, reading aloud passages from books by her favorite authors. Her hair had grown back in, bright red, like mine. Her room, kept steamy by a humidifier, sent out a whispery sound and a soft stream of steam. As she slipped in and out of awareness, her eyes would veil over with pain. I shared familiar poems like Millay's "My candle burns at both ends, it will not last the night. But ah, my foes, and oh, my friends - It gives a lovely light!" My mother finally succumbed to throat cancer and died on September 24, 1978, at age 69.

I recently found this letter that Mom wrote to me when she was aware that she didn't have long to live, which showed that she, too, was a "paper keeper":

> *[I] just had an attack of all the things I've left undone. Please don't be in too much of a rush to reorganize and get rid of what may seem like chaotic stuff. I even have copies I made of my mother and fathers' early letters to each other. Much treasured stuff. Even if this house has to be emptied to rent or sell, may there be room in a corner of that splendid big house for a file or a carton or so for awhile?*

~

As a teacher, I was eager to keep learning, so in the summer of 1979, I took a Northeastern University anthropology course, which focused on varied theories of male/female gender roles. It was taught by Mary Anne Wolff, who later wrote me a recommendation when I was applying for college jobs:

> *...Outside of the classroom, she remains a teacher in the best sense of the word, gently provoking those around her to think more clearly and doing so with wit and humility characteristic of one who exposes her own thoughts to considerable scrutiny.*

That same year, Jon and I hiked in the Arizona desert, falling deeper in love with desert flowers: Jon with their colors, I with their shapes. While Jon would take dozens of photographs with his camera's various lenses, I wanted to just sit and stare.

We also went on a backpack trip in the Colorado Rockies, the Tetons and Wind Rivers (Wyoming) with Maxime, Brigitte, and Susan Michaelis. Our French friends brought spices, pans, and the cooking expertise to create gourmet meals in the wilderness. We camped for 21 days straight, hiking 80 miles over 8 days. We fell in love with high mountain flowers we'd never seen before. We crossed high peaks and descended into valleys, unaware that a hiker on a peak near us had been killed by lightning. My metatarsal arch "fell" so I ended the trip in pain.

Meanwhile, Ben was volunteering for an Appalachian trail maintenance trip with ten hardy young people. His work involved carrying heavy wooden-framed packs and doing strenuous work, but he learned about the environment and wilderness conservation. Anthony stayed home: he wasn't willing to give up his newspaper delivery job.

Home Base School

After leaving Pilot School in 1973, I had taken "assertiveness training" courses and workshops, offered mostly to women to help them stand up for themselves. I took a few different versions: one was a 7-hour *Assertiveness Training for People Who Work with People* and another was with the Cambridge Center for Adult Education. I absorbed books like *The New Assertive Woman* ("How to know what you feel, say what you mean, and get what you want"). The training must have worked, because my evaluations from my next job at Home Base praised me for my "assertiveness and directness in dealing with students and teachers," along with my creativity, ability to listen to students, and to connect my classes to the community (and bring the community into my classes).

From 1974 to 1981, I worked at Home Base (at first as a volunteer), Watertown's public alternative high school, housed in the basement of the Armenian Cultural Center and later in an old elementary school. I started as a volunteer, was hired for a position in 1975, got tenure in 1978, and became Language Arts Director in 1981. I applied to be the English Department Chair for the whole system but I think I was out of my league and I wasn't offered the position. I also realized that I was someone that wanted to teach and share ideas and wasn't well-suited to administrative work.

Home Base was a public school that drew students who "didn't fit in" elsewhere—there were about 100 students in total. They ranged from responsible and creative to anti-social, acting out, struggling with their sexuality, or just norm-breaking (one of my male advisees felt comfortable enough to wear women's clothes and to urge me, unsuccessfully, to let him apply his make-up to my face). While the student population at Pilot was economically and culturally diverse, the Home Base kids were largely working class and had a different mix of ethnicities: many Armenian and Portuguese families; I recall there being only one Black student in the program.

Although I'd stopped running, exercise was clearly still important to me:

> *Riding my bike to Watertown [from Cambridge] and back, fighting the wind, feeling my toes and cheeks "disappear" in numbness, working out the aches I got from two gymnastics classes yesterday, steering through the sloshy streets. Pitying the insulated cars and people in them, as they, I suppose, pity me.*

After the school day, I'd often bike 10 miles from the school in Watertown to Walden Pond in Concord.

New Ideas/New Courses

I flourished in alternative schools in part because I wasn't required to teach from a textbook. My interest in languages developed into courses like *Language and Power*, *Assertiveness*, and *Debate*. My feminism evolved into a *Women's Studies* course, co-led with Gene Thompson. I thought up new courses each semester: *Book a Week Club*, *Peer Support Group* (where students could discuss their personal problems), a "habit control" class (with anti-smoking materials from American Cancer Society), a nutrition class, theater arts class, essay class, and a non-credit girls-only quilting group. I co-taught a class on the environment with science teacher Mark Petricone, and an outdoors/English course called *Survival* with our industrial arts teacher (who also led hiking/camping outings) Bert Hirtle. Although it was a lot of work to continually be experimenting and teaching new courses, the energy and excitement of working on them fueled me.

With Joe McDonald, I taught a class called *Working*, open to all four grades. We read *Working*, by the oral historian Studs Terkel, looked at historical conditions of work, and visited a GM plant, CBS-TV, Peter Bent Brigham hospital, Stride Rite, a baker, and the Raytheon corporation. We spoke to United Farm Workers organizers about the grape boycott. Some students, on their own, looked into Watertown grocers and persuaded six of them to not carry grapes (the next week, they found only one had followed through).

In a letter to my father, I wrote:

> *I am now wondering how you felt about your jobs: feelings of alienation or the usefulness of your work, relations with bosses, experiences trying to change work conditions feelings about times you were unemployed, feelings about retirement, advice to kids looking for jobs.*
> *What were you like as a boss over people who worked "under" you?*
> *Do you think schools should be doing something different to prepare students for the work world?*

Have you ever seen women who have more capability than their jobs allow them to use?
Do you think women SHOULD work?
Is there any job you think women SHOULDN'T do?
You see, this course has made me ask a lot of questions. I don't have many answers, but I have lots of questions.

In my *Cultures* class, I drew on the anthropology course I'd taken and on my experiences in other countries. I tried to broaden kids' experiences to be able to look at the world from more than one viewpoint, to analyze misunderstandings, biological/cultural issues, family norms, individual personalities.

In one assignment I had them list a behavior they didn't understand or didn't like (of a family friend teacher, or group of people) and then try to imagine the point of view of that other person or group. Other areas were: the practice of Muslim or Hindu purdah, approaches to healing, foods of different cultures, varying attitudes toward personal space, child care, kibbutzes, defining what is desirable in women or men, arranged marriages, foreigners' attitudes to Americans, Native American berdache, Jewish bris, taboos, puberty rites, vision quests, and smoking.

I wrote to my mother about my frustrations:

I am frustrated that they can identify with Samoans in the South Pacific but not blacks in Roxbury or "sleazy girls" from Watertown's projects. So busy building their own identities by putting down other people.

Teaching for me is circling in on that aspect of a "subject" which can be useful and thought-provoking for every student's life. I am always searching for that bullseye in the middle where the subject and the students' needs meet.

My *Language and Power* class explored bias (race, gender, homophobia), lying, statistics, IQ test biases, and more.

I taught *Great American Writers* to college-bound kids, writing to my mother about my students' legitimate frustrations:

> *I find these "great writers" (Faulkner, Hemingway, etc) are more interested in morbid despair than human beings in a positive way. Also they are very elitist: the working class kids in my class just can't identify with them, and I don't blame them. We need new writers with a new vision.*

I offered mini-courses in spelling, vocabulary, grammar, and SAT prep as electives. I wrote an article for the *Watertown Press* about the teenagers' enthusiasm and interest in those classes: both because they were taught in a fun way and because they were chosen by, not required of, the students.

Inspiring teenagers to write was my forte. I believed that writing should be a process (not one draft and then fix the typos, but actually reworking a piece), and should be done for an audience you care about (so the whole class gave feedback, not just the teacher). I believed in showing students both "famous" poems and poems by unknowns (including high school age poets) and exposing them to diverse topics (love, or war, or cars), so that they will feel inspired, but not pressured to copy any particular style—to use their own.

I also gave them hands-on experiences for inspiration, taking them outside to write and having them write about photographs of scenes or objects. I brought in collections of fruits they knew and ones they didn't and had them "write a poem while you are smelling, looking, cutting up and tasting a fruit or vegetable. Pretend you ARE the fruit, then write about the fruit and yourself at the same time." I completed almost every writing assignment along with them—including their essays, short stories, "how-tos," and opinion pieces—which resulted in writings of mine like:

Growing Up a Girl

We all wore push-up bras
A rib once poked up
over my prom dress
an antenna, checking out
how I was doing getting dance partners

I brought in professional poets and at the end of each course distributed a "published" booklet of of the students' work. I gave a talk at the Cambridge Alternative Alliance (of alternative schools) on using interviews in the classroom and did a similar talk on how I taught poetry. I continued to write poems, maybe 50 in all, but submitted only one (about a loon on a lake). I left the genre to "real poets," especially my sister-in-law, Gail Mazur whose poems are nuanced, but don't need a seminar to be understood.

WHILE I WAS at Home Base, I was also hired to work on an EDCO-sponsored WALSE (water, air, land, sea education) environmental curriculum. For WALSE, science teacher Mark Petricone and I developed sections of an environmental textbook, which was published in 1977. The WALSE program director, Maureen Oates, wrote me a recommendation, praising me as "provocative, resourceful, alert and involved, dependable and cheery, a terrific person to work with." At the time, I thought "Wow - me?"

I also worked on an EDCO media arts program. The music teacher and I took kids to Boston to be part of the Metropathways program, which was an urban, suburban, interracial, multilingual, intercultural arts and career awareness program led by Jose Masso and Libby Shufro. Part of the program took place at the Elma Lewis School of Fine Arts in Roxbury. I was so into "honest feedback" that I gave them three pages of it (I still have a paper copy). I praised the dance programs in my feedback, but wished that "...one session had been in a Hispanic or Haitian center so that the students would absorb more by osmosis." I also point out an instance of disrespectful stereotyping when they told one of my "pretty" girl students that she would be the one playing the hooker. Among my eleven-point critiques were these:

The "making-up culture" activity met a lot of resistance from students, so we teachers had to force them to participate/energize themselves. I enclose a role-play which might have been better to do...

Break the groups into pairs or threes more than you did. Each Spanish or Haitian student could teach another student one phrase in their language, or one dance step, or one recipe or one song...

Get written feedback after the first week, which you could then address in the second week. For instance, several girls resented that "no American culture" was represented...

I felt we were in this together and there was a sense of collegiality between us that allowed me to be as honest as possible in helping to improve this program.

Gene Thompson and I served on Watertown's Title IX Committee which ran sex equity consciousness workshops for Watertown teachers and set up a grievance procedure. We went to Washington D.C. (staying with my cousin David Colby and his wife Libba) to talk to people in different agencies about funding for women's educational curricular programs (Educational Equity Act, PEER, Women's Business & Professional Foundation, Women's Bureau, Office of Education). We were trying for a $50,000 grant for a program to teach and support girls learning non-traditional subjects but got only $2,000 from Polaroid for equipment for our women's programs, which paid for a small computer.

My experience at Home Base wasn't all positive: I encountered sexism there from one male program head. I remember him saying, as he grinned boyishly to soften the audacity of his words, "Give me a smile and I'll give you the dittos," and "When are we going out for a drink? What's the matter, are you afraid?" When he left the school, I was glad that he was replaced by a woman.

I found the cynicism of the teachers in the main high school (evidenced by teacher room talk), their apparent dislike of kids, and their pride in *not* working hard, distasteful. Our focus was on teacher collaboration, non-competitive study, and play: our Olympics featured hula hoops, juggling, and a limbo stick. Teachers and students addressed each other on a first name basis and were intent on figuring out how to help each student succeed. I wrote about this:

> *I would like to give the students I teach an attitude. More than any set of facts or skills I would like them to learn, or rather, to discover how to be curious, critical and sympathetic toward everything they experience.*

Home Base drew a certain amount of taxpayer resentment, in part because it was housed apart from Watertown High School. As a result, at one point Home Base was moved to the main high school, reduced to being a "program" and renamed "I.D.S." Then in 1981, the state passed Proposition 2 ½, which cut local taxes by 40 percent, causing school closings and "reduction-in-force" of tenured teaching jobs, including mine. But I was ready to go anyway. Although I loved teaching, I needed rejuvenation: I felt that, as a teacher, I needed to be continually learning and I needed to pursue that outside of the schools.

Soon after I stopped teaching in these progressive schools, "teaching to the test" became dominant and I've wondered ever since if my way of teaching helped or hurt my students' futures. At Home Base, grammar, spelling, vocabulary, and SAT prep were electives—should we have required them of all students?

I was gratified when, 10 years later, an ex-student of mine (Scott Hickey) called me. He'd barely made it through high school and yet wrote wonderful stories (albeit with misspellings). Scott now wanted to write a book of his own, for parents: *How to Tell If Your Kids Are on Drugs*, a topic he knew well from experience. He wanted to use his talent for story-telling that he hadn't realized he had and to help parents with recognize the signs that his parents never had.

In 2024 and 2025, two of my ex-students (from many decades ago) reached out to me with messages, both of which helped answer some questions about whether or not my approach had been helpful to my students.

My former Home Base student student Christine Lawson sent me this:

> *"Oh Barbara, you and Gene change my life. Just want you to know even if you don't remember me, you had many students I know, but I sure remember you."*

And my former Pilot School student wrote this:

> *"It's Mike Pelham. Thank you for all you did to try and guide me as a troubled youth. I was so resistant and full of fear. I always remember you with gratitude and fondness. Despite my resistance I learned a lot from you."*

Knowing that these people, now in their 60s, still held memories about my teaching helped me realize that I did indeed have a lasting positive effect.

~

Jon and I in Baja, California

Talking with student Susan Duncan at the Home Base school

6

THE PATH TO JOURNALISM

After leaving Home Base, I decided to focus on freelance writing, rather than pursuing my teaching career. I wrote to my college friend Haralyn at time:

> *I wrote all summer: articles and reviews for two women's papers, and short stories, I got it all published, earned $15. And loved it: interviewing women all over the city—the handicapped, women entrepreneurs, exercise gyms, health collectives etc. But it takes so much time to write and where's the money in it?*

As a high school teacher, I had written assignments alongside my students: in a way, I was becoming a writer through my teaching. It was the Home Base principal Joe McDonald who had urged me to submit my articles for publication. So I wrote about teaching spelling, about the exchange trip with a Vermont school, about the Soviet educators visit, career day, Olympics day, our basic skills' course, and Shakespeare. And I started to submit some of these:

I've been writing little articles for the Watertown Press about our school, to help me imagine myself capable of doing such work. I do love to write. Just putting down facts is fun for me—trying to get them into succinct form. Opinions are a little more scary.

In the early 1980s, I started regularly freelancing for the feminist women's newspaper *Equal Times.* I wrote about Gene Thompson's "Women Working" class which brought in women who worked in non-sex-stereotyped jobs. I was paid about $25 per article. The militant publisher and editor Eunice West would tell me: "You just need to get in touch with your anger."

In 1984 Eunice West closed down *Equal Times* with a goodbye note in *Sojourner: The Women's Journal,* bitterly declaring that women had gotten nowhere in the last decade. When I read her piece I reacted:

Either we're all fantasizing or she's fantastically bitter. I feel sad that the good things Equal Times did are gone (she gave no warning of the close-down, so no one got a chance to talk about buying her out), but I consider her an oddly macho feminist.

~

In the summer of 1980, we bicycle-camped with Anthony in France through Brittany and Provence. It was midsummer and very hot, but still a thrill, biking and camping for almost a month. I wrote to my father about the trip:

We biked around 500 miles in 13 days. Our muscles ached but our senses were bathed in the sight of vineyards, thick-walled farmhouses, the scent of lavender, and the taste of seafood, crackle of French bread, so hot and fresh that it made noises...

You know how you "create your own culture" on a trip? Your jokes, your habits, your appreciation of each other's little skills and weaknesses? That's what's worth the trip.

Anthony took on each pinball machine ("flipper" in French) in every café we came upon. He'd taped eight hours of his favorite music, and traveled with his tape recorder on the back of his bike, which was a great help on long hills. He learned to play boules (bocci) but never got used to the hole-in-the-ground stand-up toilets.

That same year, Ben started at Marlboro College. He wrote to his Grandfather Joe: *"I am enjoying Marlboro's countryside and academics. I am taking Economics and Environmental Science and aiming for some kind of major in politics."*

In 1981, Jon and I went to Japan, guests of Jon's colleagues, Koreaki Ito and Junko, where Jon attended a scientific conference. They wrote instructions in Japanese that allowed us to find our way around Tokyo, Kyoto, and a hotel near Mount Fuji. Anthony joined us for ten days.

I had studied Japanese for months, so I could order food and ask for directions. The culture was fascinating, but the role of women was hard to accept. I even found myself unconsciously followed "the rules" for women: walking slightly behind men, making only small gestures, continually putting on a smile. One woman revealed to us how resentful she was at her housewife role. Even when husbands returned home late, wives were expected to serve them five dishes, each prepared in a different way.

Back in the U.S., I noticed people joking, arguing, and yelling—and I joined in, glad to return to American norms. Layers of reserve that had accumulated in Japan gradually fell away. It seemed to me that the Japanese people value sensitivity to what people might be feeling or thinking, but one is expected to never say what you feel or want.

The Japan trip was one of many we would take over the next few decades where the travel and lodging expenses were paid for as part of Jon's attending a conference where he gave a talk. His scientific pursuits were creating a space for us to explore the world.

After cycling in France, Jon wanted to take a bike trip in a rural American state: we imagined small, well-maintained roads like those in rural France. In North Carolina we rented bikes, pedaling all day and camping at night. But the small roads were trafficky and off-leash dogs would run after us. When we stopped at a bike store, the guys advised us to "go to New England to bike." It turns out that North Carolina didn't have enough money to pave all of its roads, so those that were paved were heavily traveled. On our last day, wanting "to get this over with," we biked 100 miles, finishing exhausted and borderline delirious.

I JOINED sports clubs for exercise for the first time in 1982: first the YWCA, then the New England Women's gym, and later the Mount Auburn Club, the Boston Sports Club in Allston, and eventually the Concord-Acton Squash Club. By 1983, I was doing weightlifting, jogging, and swimming.

Jon and I returned to Utah that summer: its southwestern "red rock country" enthralled us so much that we went back every other year. We thought Escalante the most beautiful place we'd ever seen, like an outdoor sculpture gallery. I wrote a short article about our trip and then wrote about the process in my journal:

> *The problem with freelancing is that it is such a struggle to write without a guaranteed audience that it's hard to get done. I clearly need structure, a group of people to work with.*

The next year, we flew out to Utah in June, expecting to hike the whole time. But the snow had been heavy that year (we hadn't thought about this possibility before we left) and every mountain range we tried to hike was snowed in. We drove to Idaho, then to Montana and to Nevada, and in the end we just laughed about our fruitless search, and considered that we'd learned our lesson: check the local conditions before your trip.

It was also in 1982 that my neighbor and friend Gail Graves and her son Adam and I went to the New York City *United Nations Disarmament* rally on a Mobilization for Survival bus with (Ben went separately, but I didn't see him). I brought a cloth banner quoting my students' fears. Speakers at the Central Park rally included Linda Ronstadt, Bella Abzug, Orson Welles, Dick Gregory, Jackson Brown, and Joan Baez. Because of the crowd of 500,000-800,000, we were too far back to even see them.

For the next few years, I was active in Educators for Social Responsibility, along with Home Base teachers Gene Thompson and Joe McDonald. We collectively developed and published *Dialogue: A Teaching Guide to Nuclear Issues* (c.1982), and a second one, *Perspectives: A Teaching Guide to Concepts of Peace* (1983). We also held workshops.

I tried to start jogging again, but I worried about back pain (I had stopped for a few years: maybe my 6.2 mile daily runs were too much for my body to withstand).

A Toe in Journalism

JUST LIKE WITH TEACHING JOBS, I found my freelancing "niche" on the second try, in the mid- to late-1980s. *Sojourner* wanted me to write regularly and they published my "news notes" and feature stories on topics like "Bringing Up Boys Not to be Men," "Sonia Johnson runs for President," "Carrie Dearborn - Sitdown Comic," and "Women Working in Progressive Male-dominated Organizations."

I joined *Sojourner's* editorial group, where I was the oldest woman there. I remember that at one meeting, when I said my age, everyone turned around to stare. But I was accepted and appreciated: I wrote features, interviews, and book reviews (about $15 an article) and was their volunteer news editor. My journal reflected both my tendency towards self-criticism and that I was growing as a writer:

> *I just finished an article for Soj but as soon as I handed it in, I felt what I really wanted to say well up inside me. I wanted to call up, say stop the typeset machine! I've changed my mind—that's not what I want to say at all! I didn't call. The best part of journalism is for me the finality of having an article in print.*
>
> *My prose might lurch at points, may wander off into vagaries, may merely skim the surface of what there is to say, but when it's done, it's done. It's set in print, on the newsstand, in the hands of people I know or don't know read and liked, or scorned. But it can't be taken back. It may be raw and need more cooking, but I now can see where I am. I took a topic that troubles me, fascinates me, describes me: feminists with boys.*
>
> *When I started interviewing mothers of boys, I went too fast. I was startled by what they gave me: sweetness and light. I probed with the dullest of sticks and they shrank back from my probe. "My son is so sensitive and loving, so non-sexist." What I got was black and white, while the truth is usually grey. The grey was the reason I chose the topic in the first place.*
>
> *I am in fear and trembling trying to write a book review of a book called Personal Politics, which describes the origin of women's moving rising out of the Civil Rights and anti-war moment. I want to send it to one of the women's newspapers because I am trying to imagine myself "a reporter."*

In the mid-1980s, I joined a feminist writing group, a mix of lesbian, straight, and bisexual women, some of whom later started the New Words women's bookstore. The dominant figure was

Barbara McDonald, who would rail against unintended homophobia or ageism in our writing. In my journal, I wondered about the degree of her fury and asked myself: "Could rage be a gift? Or is it an abuse of power that we hate in men, and must not use ourselves?"

The group did inspire me to dare to write and submit a piece on an incident that I might not have otherwise risked publishing. As a young graduate student in the early 1960s, I'd accepted a ride home from a guy I had met at Hays Bickford café. He drove to the underpass by Cambridge Rindge and Latin and forced me into oral sex. At the time, I'd blamed this humiliating experience on my being stupid, gullible, or sluttish. I now understood that it was not my fault: it was rape.

I TRIED to be creative in my article ideas, one of which was to interview twenty Huron Avenue women store-owners (the stores were just a few blocks from our home) for one hour each and write about their experiences. I brought the resulting sprawling article to the *Cambridge Chronicle*'s Central Square office. I remember the piles of paper on the editor's desk, and the tiny cockroaches running through them. The weekly's editor, David Weigand, told me to shape my article more, and when I brought it back he published it—my first "feature article," in November of 1981. He also ran my humorous piece about jaywalking in Harvard Square, including black-and-white photos of the throngs crossing against the light in front of Out of Town News.

I wrote other articles for this same editor: *Biking to Walden Pond, Biking to Nahant, On Learning Russian, CRLS Student Programmed for Success,* and *CRLS with an International Flavor.* I wrote to a friend:

> *I am putting my toe in journalism. It is freezing but I like the cold. I like being around adults. I like creating instead of*

helping other people create. I like interviewing people, digging up facts, juggling words, handing in a finished product and then forgetting about it.

I then pitched ideas to the *Cambridge Tab*. I wrote articles on *Economic Conversion: Creating an Alliance for Jobs*, and *Reading, Writing and Rebates: Will Merit Teacher Pay Work?* I loved popping into a newspaper to hand my articles to the editor. I wrote that I especially loved *"...breathing in the smoke-filled newspaper atmosphere the whole time as if it were fresh bread."*

At the same time, I was writing social-political articles for *Science for the People*, like "How Magazines Cover Sex Difference Research: Journalism Abdicates its Watchdog Role", "Teaching Peace," and "Science for Human Rights: Using Genetic Screening and Forensic Science to Find Argentina's Disappeared."

Becoming "A Professional"

In 1982, I took a "first-person essay course" from Mopsy Strange Kennedy at the Cambridge Center for Adult Education. The course made me want to write more personal essays, in contrast to the straight journalism I'd been doing. Mopsy enthusiastically praised my personal pieces and delighted in my wry humor. Her praise made me realize that humor *is* a natural part of my writing style. I started to embrace it:

I wrote this heavy bitter thing about dad and now I've rewritten it so it will be funny. Am I deserting feminism if I take a light and humane attitude to Dad? I think not.

I think a sense of humor makes me happy! Bitter is Boring.

At the same time, I also became determined to "go professional" as a journalist, and to do so, I needed "credentials," meaning training and a degree. I wrote to Dad:

I gradually realized that if I want to apply for a job at a newspaper, I want to really KNOW that I know what I'm doing. Without that background, I won't have the nerve to apply, especially at the age of 44.

Boston University offered a one-year master's in Print Journalism program with strong hands-on elements, including a half year "on the beat" and a chance to write several lengthy magazine articles for publication.

I wrote about my back-to-school move in *Sojourner,* with this lead: "Why would a feminist want to go into journalism—a field dominated by men and losing ground daily to the expanding world of video?"

Why am I, at age 45 and after 11 years as a high school teacher, switching to journalism?

First of all, I like to write. I also like to ask questions of people unlike me, and this is a good excuse. And as a feminist, I see journalism as a chance to network ideas and information that can galvanize women to new thinking and action. We women don't get our fair share of news space. We make up half the population but we don't get half the news.

Editors may say we must hold traditional positions of power or we're not newsworthy. I say that as long as we don't hold those positions of power, our fair share of newsprint should go towards analyzing why. And toward networking ideas and information that can change that imbalance in power. I want to be part of that process.

I was probably (again) the oldest person in the program, the same age as some of my professors, which helped me speak up when I saw something I didn't like, starting with the booklist we were sent to prepare us for the program.

When I saw that the list had only male authors, I researched and wrote up a list of female-authored journalism books and asked my professor to distribute it to everyone. The male department head, said "point well taken" and that he'd make copies to give to the women professors. I complained in my journal that "The women profs don't need them!" but admitted to myself that "I didn't think fast enough to say that."

I biked to and from Boston University daily, completed every assignment, read every assigned book, and missed not one class, while the younger students seemed to look for every excuse to skip. I wrote with dismay about the program itself, as well:

> *The system doesn't encourage networking, dialoguing, sharing resources! As Joe said of Harvard—it "de-adulticizes" you fast. I'm used to being treated, when teaching or working with Sojourner, as a co-worker. Part of it is that no one knows me, or cares to. All they care about is what they can tell me. I am the empty jar for what THEY will fill?*

At times, I felt oddly infantalized. My first City Desk assignment was to write my own obituary (in 15 minutes). When the professor said "very good" as she returned mine, I found myself clinging to her remark like an elementary school kid who's been handed a gold star.

Yet I also critiqued (in my journal) my journalism professors:

> *Doesn't anyone in college know how to teach? To get inside the heads of those they are trying to change? Couldn't more have been done to help C. catch on to newsroom style? Couldn't the law profs have passed out a syllabus, explained how to track down case law?*

I was forced to use a computer for the first time, and kept pushing the wrong key, which shut down the entire roomful of computers (they were all connected back then), infuriating my professor. Five years later, I embraced writing by computers: I wrote to my father that "being able to write on such a handy machine makes a huge difference. You can revise and revise until it's perfect. I couldn't do without it."

IRONICALLY, although I wrote in my journal that my goal was "...to bring out the women's half of the news. If there doesn't seem to be any, to spend that half on analyzing the dynamics of why there isn't," I got my first rejection from *Sojourner*.

It seems that in learning to write "straight news." I'd diminished my feminist sensibility. I was also aware that my fellow "journalists-in-training" were more ambitious than I. As I wrote in my journal:

> *Ambition can compromise you, masculinize me, while feminism has nourished in me. Hopefully I will be nourished before it swallows me.*

Two professors *did* nourish me. Bernice Buresh's *Woman and Minorities* course led me to research the range and type of coverage (biased and objective) of 10 newspapers' reports of the December 1982 shooting of a young black man by a policeman in Miami and the looting and car burning and police response that followed. Caryl Rivers, who taught magazine writing, encouraged me to submit what I wrote to newspapers or magazines.

All of the articles I wrote were on social justice issues (one on teachers who taught nuclear arms issues, another on a community organizer, a third on advocacy organizations). The most substantive article I wrote in this class was on how sociobiology in magazines such as *Cosmopolitan, Playboy,* and *Reader's Digest* ascribed rape to competition. The article was published in the *Columbia Journalism Review*, which helped me later because I could cite work of mine appearing in such a prestigious publication. At first, the *CJR* editor had thought it was interesting but a "mess" and wanted me to work with an MIT professor. But she'd just had twin kids whose similarities changed her attitude toward sociobiology. So I re-wrote the article on my own and it was accepted.

But the *CJR* article also led to my first serious stumble as a professional journalist. I'd sent my original draft not only to *CJR* but also to a competing national journalism publication, *The Quill*. Both wanted it. The *Quill* editor, who hadn't communicated for months as I worked with *CJR* on edits, corrections, and proofreading, was furious with me. I meekly apologized but later was told that since the *Quill* editor had never offered me a contract, I had no obligation to him.

Looking for a Beat

My City Desk professor urged me to do my "practice beat" as an environmental or other topic-specific reporter, but I insisted on a "general city beat"—I wanted to cover "the people." I called various newspapers, seeking a temporary position: the *Quincy Patriot Ledger* immediately assigned me to cover local events. But I soon switched to the *Middlesex News*, whose Waltham bureau suburban daily editor, Vicky Ogden, was impressed that I had clippings to show:

> *The editor said she'd see me, even though her quota of students, arranged with B.U, was filled. She looked at my resume, asked what Equal Times was, then looked at my 35 clips. She made interested noises and said she liked my stuff and said "this is good—I can tell because I keep wanting to read every article."*

She signed me on as a Waltham Bureau "stringer" for $20 an article, so I was both a stringer and a B.U. student at the same time. For nine months, I covered calendar listings, the police & crime beat, minor committee meetings, and "fun" features. The part of daily journalism that I loved the most was having to go off somewhere new to talk to someone you'd never met before and to interview that person about a topic you knew little about.

To write well is to be yourself and your reader. I try to be inside and outside my work, to know how it will seem. I am only partway there.

I wrote "hard news" with headlines like: "Cemetery Board and Environmentalists Clash over Brook," "Asbestos Found in High School," "Dangers of Affirmative Action Outlined," "He's Fighting to Allow Women in All-Male Club" and "Creative Solution Needed for Toxic Waste," but I think I was not as driven as other reporters who needed to support themselves. At one point, I was deeply disturbed at the excited announcement by another (female) reporter about a new assignment: "Oh boy, a rape!" She knew it would get on the front page and advance her career. I couldn't believe that the opportunity to get on the front page seemed more important to her than the impact on the rape victim.

I liked the constant challenge of meeting new people (reporter and editor Jan Gardner became my good friend for the rest of my life) and new experiences I had every day. I even liked staying up until 3 a.m. writing up evening meetings. When the editor dressed me down on a mistake (the budget that the School Committee voted on), I wrote down what I had to learn:

There's nothing to do but go on—the virtue of a daily newspaper is that you have to. And that 'no one's perfect'... I'm in trouble if I think everyone but myself makes mistakes...

I did not like the hectic pace, however: you had to do everything fast and yet at the same time get all of your facts straight. Nor did I like the narrowness of what you are allowed to explore and write about. Also, at that age, the hours and deadlines could be grueling. I wrote to my father:

> *It's hard to cover a meeting and then go right back to the bureau and type out the article directly from my notes. I'd get home between 1:30 and 3:30 a.m. but it's exciting, just trying to get all the facts straight and it's a test of whether we can "write under deadline."*
>
> *I do police news, which is scary—I need to be completely accurate since I'm dealing with people's reputations. I also do community news: I like it best when I'm sent out on the spur of the moment—grab the camera and run.*

DESPITE THE CHALLENGES of the job, in August of 1983 I applied for full-time jobs at the *Medford Daily News* (no openings) the *Waltham News Tribune* (no openings), and the *Dedham Transcript* (offered me a job). I was offered a job by *Globe Pequot Press* to research Massachusetts B&Bs and hotels. I turned that one down, since it required intensive travel for months and I'd have to talk my way into the place I was reviewing to give me free room and board, which the publisher wouldn't pay for, which felt ethically compromising.

I finally accepted an offer for a "real job" as a reporter at the *Brookline Chronicle*. As a weekly, I thought that it would be lower-key than the *Middlesex News*. But I was one of just two reporters who had to cover everything (city government, police and courts, education). The other reporter had the knack of sleeping through most of the long meetings and then waking for agenda items she needed to write on.

I learned to write my story *during the meeting*, and to approach politicians later to get quotes on the story I'd already decided on. I was writing three articles a week. I made mistakes but learned to plow on: at one point, I thought I had a scoop when I saw deteriorating steps in public housing and reported on it without giving the head of the housing project an opportunity to respond to the charge. He called and dressed me down for unfair reporting.

I relished doing articles on social issues: interviewing caregivers for "Hospice Helps the Whole Family," reporting on various school committee issues, on condo conversions, the hidden costs of town meetings, on how to keep heating costs down, student reactions to "The Day After" (a film on life after a nuclear war by the Brookline Action for Nuclear Disarmament), U.S. Representative Barney Frank's foreign policy (tough to gets sound bites from him), and articles like "All in a Day's Police Work" and "Soviet Students Tell of Life They Left Behind."

Despite the pressure of the job, working on a deadline did make me feel productive—and like a real "working stiff."

~

Some of the articles I had published

7
CHAFING AT THE HIERARCHY

In October of 1983, the United States military invaded Grenada, "rescuing" American medical students from a small Caribbean island that had been over overthrown by a communism-friendly group. President Reagan declared the airstrip that they were building was "a Soviet-Cuban threat." I had to finish a half-dozen articles for that week's edition of the paper and so I couldn't join in demonstrations against this military action, the first of its kind since the end of the Vietnam War. Only the typesetter and I took the time to call our senators and congresspeople.

I realized that I couldn't count on others to protest what I thought was wrong, so I quit my job and became a freelancer so I could be free to protest my country's military aggressions (my Globe editor friend Jan was not allowed to be political in any way—no protest letters, demonstrations, or membership in any organizations, including the National Writers Union).

But there were other reasons. In a letter to a friend, I wrote that I left because "I didn't much like being bossed around" (we had to punch out every time we left the building and then punch in when we returned, like factory workers). I wrote to my feminist writing group: "I left after a few months, chafing at the hierarchy, the lack of autonomy, the disconnection with what I care about, the mindless pace." And I wrote to another friend:

> *After 3 months at the Brookline Chronicle, I quit. Too little control. Too much tension, too little exercise, etc. I'm sorry, though—I thought I'd like working for a local paper and that I'd want to do it for years.*
>
> *Now I'm wallowing around in my free time like both a happy hippo and a quicksand-victim-to-be.*

As a fledgling journalist with only a year of "hard news" experience, I returned to freelancing. To "learn the ropes" from fellow freelancers, I joined the National Writers Union, started a "career support group" of union members to focus on pushing each other to the next step, and was elected to the Boston Chapter Steering Committee.

Between 1984 and 1988, I wrote and published articles in local publications ($15-$200 per article), and eventually in 20 national newspapers and magazines ($200-$1500 per article). The *Boston Globe* assigned me education articles.

I was able to successfully pitch my ideas to newspapers such as the *Baltimore Sun, Christian Science Monitor, Oakland Tribune, Metrowest Extra, Whole Life Times, Cambridge Chronicle,* and *The Somerville Journal.* I also was able to get published in magazines like *Ms., Women and Health, Adirondack Life, Science for the People, Labor Notes*, *Wellesley Magazine,* and *Essence.*

Despite my publishing success, my father would have chided me for my "jumping around" habit. After I'd publish in a prominent magazine, I'd move on to a different publication rather than sticking with the one where I already had connections. Looking back, it seems like I wanted to rack up an impressive number of publications for my resume. I probably should have focused on a few.

I turned down several opportunities: I wrote for *Index on*

Censorship and then was asked to be its regular columnist, but I didn't want to limit myself to just one issue. l was offered a job writing a book on women's health issues, but I didn't feel capable at that point of writing a full-length book.

I mostly wrote on social justice issues, sometimes for little or no money, in *Dollars and Sense, Peaceworks, New Mobility, American Writer, Rough Draft,* and *Maine in Print.* I wrote in my diary:

> *I am surprised at the simple joy I get of just seeing my name in print. Like a child, I think. Only then comes the worry that no one else will read it, or that I'll never know anyone who did.*

I sometimes heard from my readers: when I wrote an article for *Wellesley Magazine* on why I felt driven to do civil disobedience, alums wrote letters protesting my civil disobedience article. But I also got personal letters from five alumni who thanked me for it. Best of all, my brother-in-law Peter said that while reading the article, he cried.

Still, I struggled with "who am I?" questions, as in this excerpt from an essay for my fellow union member writers:

> *The longer I write, the harder it is to answer the question: What do you do? "I'm a writer" never satisfies. "What do you write?" always follows, and then I'm stuck. Do I answer by topic, by genre, by decade? Do I extract from my 20-year writing life, my most impressive publications, where my work appeared just once, and long ago? Or do I cite my most recent acceptance by a sports magazine that pays little and is read by few? Or should I share the piece I'm writing now, a work-in-progress, the point of which I am not yet clear?*
>
> *It's surely easier if you're a doctor or a dot-commer. Such jobs everyone can picture; if you say you're a writer, your conversational counterpart may have only a vague notion of what that means, and will most probably insist you fill in him or her.*

"Whatever interests me," I've tried replying, and offer a stream of topics like a tray of canapes for which to choose the tastiest. My current list goes like this: hiking in the desert, oral history with my father, changing personalities when I go to France, talking loud, guns and my grandsons, squash as metaphor (I explain that I mean the sport, not the vegetable).

If I've had a drink, I may proffer more provocative topics like sexual sculptures on Romanesque churches, or not knowing where my cervix is, or growing up white and oblivious, which is guaranteed to stun them into silence. If I name my top publications, I'll be asked "oh, are you famous? Should I know you?" I shift the focus: "Actually, I'm spending most of my time promoting my husband's memoir. I'm the writer and he's the author, heh, heh."

My hard work in journalism was balanced by our continuing hiking and bicycling adventures. We went on a bike-camping trip in France in 1984 with our friends Steve Burden and Susan Michaelis, but discovered that our passions differed: Jon and I wanted to see every Romanesque church in the area, while Steve wanted to visit castles. Jon decided that he would bike on his own up to a hill-top church.

On his way back, as he rode down the steep hill, he took his hand off the brakes to take off his cap. The other hand gripped the front brakes too hard and he flew over the top of the handlebars, breaking his arm. Despite being the most experienced bicyclist of the four of us, he had cared more about losing his hat than keeping control of his bike. A drunk guy at a café wrested the twisted bike wheel back into shape with this hands, and Jon was able to get his arm treated at a hospital for next to no cost.

Before his mishap, Jon and I had gathered information for an article we would publish together on "gourmet bicycling."

We wrote about how we'd ride our bikes all day, set up our tents, get sweaty, but then put on fancy clothes and go to restaurants that required reservations. Our co-written article was published in *Ford Times* magazine and also in a Boston-area newspaper.

THE FOLLOWING YEAR, Jon took a sabbatical in Berkeley, California in 1985, so I went with him. We drove across the country via New Orleans (crawfish jambalayas!) and Big Bend National Park, where we hiked. For the four sabbatical months, we lived at 417 Vassar St. (a professor's house) in the Berkeley hills, while Jennifer and Nick, my niece and nephew, stayed in our Cambridge house.

Jon worked at the Berkeley lab, while I got writer's block. For the first time, I found myself unable to complete articles that I'd gotten the go-ahead for from *Sojourner,* including one on the Cuban education system. The absence of connections with other writers in Berkeley—something that had been so important to me in Cambridge—stymied me. It was also sunny and beautiful almost every day, so I felt obliged to be out of the house all the time. In the end, I told Jon I needed to just take a break from writing.

So instead of writing during those four months, I biked a lot in the hilly areas above Berkeley and Oakland, went for hikes in local hills, and read 72 books. Ben and Anthony visited and joined us on these treks. At the same time, I generally felt worse about myself and even developed a kind of "panic attack" phobia while I was there. I wrote:

> *I've developed a psychosomatic fear of bridges. Maybe it has something to do with all the perfect weather—being an Easterner it seems immoral not to go out and play on a sunny day... it drives me outside. I can't wait to get back* [to Cambridge] *and am planning to apply for a job teaching writing at the*

college level... Writing and teaching writing should go well together.

My need for a project led to me becoming politically involved in the Bay Area. I joined protests of President Reagan's policies in Nicaragua and El Salvador. Reagan had just announced an embargo of Nicaragua after President Ortega asked the USSR for $200 million in aid. I was one of 300 arrested (including Daniel Ellsberg) in San Francisco at the federal building. In court, we acted as our own defense, basing our arguments on international law that prohibits weapons that would kill innocent populations. I was charged with trespassing and received probation.

Around the same time, 50,000 people marched in protest of Reagan's aid to the Contras of Nicaragua. Berkeley's Socialist mayor and its city council protested police using choke-holds when arresting students. The University of California at Berkeley students held a 27-day student sit-in to pressure (successfully) the university to divest from South Africa.

My interest in art was still strong and so I took a “primitive art” course in Berkeley, which led me to fall in love with African sculpture.

In 1985, Jon was diagnosed with “mitral valve prolapse” and was told that he could no longer hike at high altitudes. I remember holding each other and wondering if we'd survive as a couple without our summer backpack trips in high mountains that were so mutually invigorating. Happily, we also loved Utah's lower-elevation Red Rock wilderness, which we'd go back to every other year until 2014.

In 1986, Jon was invited to Cuba, whose government wanted help building its biology products industry. We spent much of the time escorted around, but got to spend a little time on our own. It was a fascinating trip: the only men who asked us to exchange Cuba's currency for dollars were dark-skinned. One light-skinned taxi driver openly and angrily called another driver the N-word, yet a dark-skinned biologist told Jon he would never have been able to become a scientist under the racist Battista regime.

On a second trip to Cuba, in 1988, the government arranged for me to visit schools and to interview poet and professor Nancy Morejon. I never produced an article on Cuban writers as I had planned, but I did publish an article on the Cuban schools for two newspapers.

After returning home to Cambridge, I was determined to get past my writer's block by going to a therapist. To find one, I first paid for a single session with four different therapists. I chose Susan Schenkel in part because she'd written a book, *Giving Away Success*, about women like myself who were raised in the 1950s by stay-at-home moms who modeled giving of themselves, not getting for themselves. I felt she would push me to get through whatever was stopping me.

One of my main issues had to do with money. I'd never made much of it, especially compared with Jon's salary. But I also knew that I didn't have the economic pressure to get a job. I would often compare myself to Gene Thompson and Jan Gardner, who were focused and ambitious, while I would feel somehow inauthentic. I was a feminist but never tried to—or needed to—handle our household financial accounts. I admired the idea of the "working stiff," but I knew that I was not one. I worried that if Jon had a heart attack, I wouldn't know how to support myself. But I would fantasize about learning how to deal with the finances because I'd be forced to.

I was oblivious to the therapy conventions: I showed up with my 10-page analysis of what my problems were, and was surprised that she didn't want to read it and instead wanted me to talk it all out. In my list, I had included a list of article ideas I wanted to write (listing them must have helped because I can now see that of 16 story ideas, I ended up publishing twelve of them).

I was clear about my values:

> *I like to share what I know with people, to contribute, to give people the information they need to think and act.*

I was unclear about what my problem was:

> *Often, I get depressed that I am depressed. What right have I to be depressed? I have every advantage in the world. So I feel worse."*

My issue seemed to be that I felt badly that Jon was high-status and paid well. I was hung up on Jon's fame and felt unconfident as a writer. I'd intended to go to therapy for just a few weeks, but ended up going for an entire year.

Schenkel's "rational therapy" approach worked well—it got me to name the worst that could happen and then "de-catastrophize" ("so what if you fail?"). She convinced me that there was no need to compare myself to others or to be bothered by my image of how others might view me, absent evidence. She encouraged me to find answers to my obsessive thoughts, to decide what I wanted to change, and to record how I did so. After a year, I considered myself ready to apply that perspective to my life, which I have done ever since.

At one point I wrote about writing as both therapy and *not* therapy:

> *A subject spins out of me, like a spider spins a single thread from its belly, then crafts it into a web. The journey from self-absorbed worry to some kind of perspective.*

Not that the issues facing me and other freelancers went away. Around this time, I wrote to my sister Linda:

Now I see what it must be like to be a freelance artist like Peter. You put all this energy into something without knowing just who your audience is OR whether anyone in the end is going to want to read or pay for it. Writing is better and worse than painting—better because you can always DEMAND that someone read it by sticking it in a newspaper they read by habit.

I just wrote these articles for the local paper and thought no one had bothered to buy the paper that week but now a month later, all kinds of people are telling me they read and loved it... I hate not earning money. I feel guilty going out during the day!

I try to justify my existence by doing a lot of errands. I just joined Educators for Social Responsibility and am in a group that is making up curriculum ideas for a nationwide "day of dialogue."

Civil Disobedience, Despite the Rain

In the mid 1980s (1983 to 1986), I got deeply involved in anti-nuclear arms demonstrations and civil disobedience. The US/USSR arms race was escalating. When I had taught at Home Base, my students were certain they would die in a nuclear war. The last straw came when my neighbor's son told his mother that he'd learned in Chemistry class what two household products, if combined, could make poison; he now knew what to do "when the bomb drops."

Since Anthony was at UMass/Amherst and Ben was living and working on his own, I felt I could go to jail if I had to, without hurting my family. I joined the New England Campaign to Stop Euromissiles, as well as Mobilization for Survival (I asked the

MOB activist who wrote press releases to let me write one; she said no, not being of the mentor type).

A group of Cambridge women (myself, Gail Graves, Judy Summersby, Ros Polland, Susan Redlich, Vicky Solomon and others) started to meet for potlucks to plan civil disobedience (CD) actions to protest the arms race. We formed an "affinity group" called Protest in Peace. MOB gave training in what CD involves and scheduled a protest march at AVCO, the state's largest missile manufacturing plant in Wilmington. It produced Pershing and Cruise missiles—aggressive, first-strike missiles that we felt would tempt the USSR to put its missiles on launch warning status. These missiles were designed to evade the radar and satellite detection that would be necessary for arms control. The town of Wilmington tried to prohibit the demonstration, but a judge ruled that it must be allowed on first amendment grounds.

It was raining the day of our first protest, but dressed in slickers and boots, five of us linked hands and sat down, blocking the worker's driveway into the AVCO plant. When the police dragged us to the curb, or into a mud puddle, we walked back to the center of the driveway, again and again, like a silent tide. We kept this up for an hour and then left. I handed out a statement that said, in part:

> *"I am the mother of two draft-age boys. I have come to commit open and peaceful civil disobediençe for the first time in my life because the arms race is more dangerous now than ever before...*
>
> *"We consider our disobedience a responsible act. We protest in peace in the tradition of the suffragists, Gandhi, Martin Luther King, Susan B. Anthony, Rosa Parks, the Quakers and underground railway abolitionists, and participants in the Boston Tea Party. But unlike our Tea Party ancestors, we are ready to say our names and to disobey publicly and proudly."*

We expected to be arrested, but were not. The next month, 200 people, two-thirds of us women, showed up again at AVCO, but 250 riot-control police confronted us, along with 11 attack dogs, a row of police wagons, and a helicopter that roared above us. AVCO had erected a fence to keep us off the normally accessible lawn. So we climbed over or under the fence. Many were bashed about by police, and their dogs bit three demonstrators.

We were among 42 protestors who were arrested for trespassing, including Sonia Johnson, the Citizens Party candidate for U.S. president in the last election and spent a night in the Framingham Women's prison. At the Woburn District Court, we presented ourselves in order to "gum up the court process." With ACLU lawyers advising us, we tried, unsuccessfully, to enter a "necessary defense." I wrote to the judge to ask that out-of-state arrestees not be required to appear in person (the judge turned down my request).

I kept us all in touch with each other via a newsletter (we lived in different states), and wrote my own statement to give to the media. I and others in my affinity group met with *Boston Globe* editors to urge coverage of nuclear armament issues. I also critiqued my own civil disobedience comrades in a piece for *Boston Mobilizer* about the rude behavior of some protesters (I watched and rewatched a video of the demonstration, so I had specific incidents to back me up).

When we went to trial, one militant group refused to give their real names and faced harsher penalties. Those of us who did give our names, but refused to pay the $125 fine, faced jail time but were allowed to work off our "debt to society" by each serving 35 hours of community service.

A few months later, we again deliberately blocked entrances, this time at the Logan Hilton, where arms manufacturers and government officials were planning sales to third world countries. Our affinity group, "the Eurythmics," hung slogans on a string like laundry, including "Tell the Hilton: arms-sale conferences make bad bedfellows" and "Use your economic clout against arms sales to the third world—don't patronize the Hilton." We were arrested and jailed briefly at the Charles Street Jail. An East Boston District Court judge ordered us to do community service.

Jail was not pleasant but community service was interesting: I did voter registration at Boston City Hospital. I also dug weeds, transplanted cabbage, and picked raspberries at Neskeag cooperative farm, and helped deliver fresh produce to an East Boston farm stand.

~

One of our protesters getting arrested at AVCO, in the rain.
Photo by Ellen Shub

Calmly changing a flat while on a bicycle-camping trip in France, 1980s

8

TEACHING WRITING

In the fall of 1985, now confident in my journalism skills, I applied for a job teaching college-level journalism and expository writing. Joe McDonald (former Home Base Interdepartmental Studies coordinator) helped me out by writing a recommendation for me, observing, in part: "She likes people, and so takes a genuine interest in the stories they tell and the ideas they struggle to create."

I applied to several programs: the UMass/Boston's Freshman Writing program, the Middlesex Community College Division of Continuing Education, Bunker Hill Community College, the Tufts Department of English freshman composition position, and another at Boston University. Harvard's freshman composition program head, Richard Marius, called to ask if I wanted to be interviewed. In the end, I had to decline because by then we'd agreed to go to Cuba for our second trip and I couldn't schedule another interview before we left.

I was finally offered a job teaching *Freshman English* at Framingham State College. But at the last minute, they asked me to switch to *Introduction to Journalism* instead: the professor hadn't shown up for the first class. I was happy to do so, being told I could design my own curriculum and would be teaching journalism to students who elected the course and therefore were more motivated.

However, teaching two classes of journalism took up all of my time: my classes were held twice a week, one in the morning and one in the afternoon, and it seemed like I spent the rest of the week preparing. The head of the department kept telling me how terrific all the reports were from other teachers. At the end of the year, the department head practically begged me to stay on, full-time, if possible. But I didn't: I wanted to write more, and so I returned to what I described as "the misty sea of freelancing."

I wrote to my cousin Ann, whose published personal essays (under a pseudonym) inspired me:

How can you find the time to write if you have a full-time job?

I taught two courses last semester, was frustrated that I didn't have time to write, but now have just agreed to teach again, this time in adult education. But I feel so silly, making almost no money, and producing so little.

I spend most of my time doing unpaid work organizing our National Writers Union local. I spend more time empowering other people than doing my own writing.

From 1985 to 1988, I taught *Breaking into Print: The Basics of Freelance Writing*, an adult education course, in the Boston, Brookline and Cambridge Adult Education Centers. The pay was minimal, but teaching adults eager for what I had to offer was gratifying. When asked to teach a continuing class privately, I offered *Continued Breaking into Print* at my home, insisting that we treat each other as peers. Through this course, I met Susan Pollack and June Lemen, who, along with Edith Pearlman, started meeting monthly as an essay support group, which continued for

20 years. I probably wouldn't be writing and publishing if it weren't for the feedback and encouragement and shared resources of these three fellow writers.

In the late 1980s, I started to look for a job as a professional organizer, assuming that my union experience would qualify me. I applied for a Somerville-Cambridge Elder Services PR position, Brookline's "Publishing for Literacy" project coordinator, a State House Watch staff writer position (Mass Human Services Coalition), Physicians for Social Responsibility membership officer (they interviewed me), and Massachusetts Civil Liberties Union-Bill of Rights Education Program (they interviewed me).

I was looking for a way to work with people that had the same values as I and maybe I was hoping to see if I could do the kind of work that my dad was so adept at. But, had I gotten one of these jobs, would I have "risen to the occasion"? I'm not sure. I had done a good job organizing in the union and I thought that skill would have been transferrable, but in the union I knew the people so well. I realized that in the positions I was applying for, I would have been working *for* powerful people, carrying out *their* vision, rather than collaborating with them, the opposite of my experience in the NWU. I left some of the interviews feeling like it just wasn't a good fit and that perhaps I didn't have the skills to match their needs. My organizing skills *were* valued by the National Writers Union and I kept being re-elected to do that gratifying work.

I was elected co-chair of the Boston chapter of the National Writers Union, but at one point stepped down from co-chair position to work (for pay) as the chapter's administrator. I continued as co-chair and later returned to the National Board and earned a stipend as Eastern Organizing VP and then Internal Organizing VP.

By this time, Jon and I had devoted ourselves to regular trips to the Utah Wilderness. In 1987, we hiked Utah's Grand Gulch Paria Horseshoe Canyon, which proved to be our last *overnight* backpacking trip. The weight of the backpack caused my metatarsal arch to fall, making hiking painful, even on flat surfaces. Jon and I continued to travel to Utah to hike, but switched to early morning day hikes and hotel rooms at night, which turned out to be more enjoyable than backpacking and camping out—if less macho.

In 1988, I went on a 16-day Educators for Social Responsibility tour of the USSR. We went to a pioneer youth camp, to Leningrad, Pskov, Vilnius and Kaunas (Lithuania), and Moscow. The trip also included a "roundtable" meeting with teachers. I'd studied the language for a year so I was able to wander on my own. I managed to talk with Russians in a bookstore. I tried out the term "spasibo" ("thank you") on the bus driver and it worked. Then I tried to say "Is it always so hot?" but it came out as "Is everyone so hot?" But I did understand when he said "prokhladnyy" (cool). Despite my missteps, it gave me a good feeling to interact with people through language in this far-away country.

In Vilnius, young people invited two of us to their homes, and told us where Jews had been slaughtered by Nazis and buried in trenches in the woods. Other Jewish people talked of the art they were collecting for safe keeping. When I returned home, I mailed one Russian teacher a box of contemporary novels, but she never got them: they'd been confiscated or stolen.

My resulting article about education in the Soviet Union was published in the *Christian Science Monitor*. I learned from Linda and Peter (my sister and brother-in-law, who subscribe to the newspaper) that they had read it, were impressed by its even-handedness, and only then noticed that it was I who had written it. A newspaper freelancer rarely hears from readers, so it was gratifying to hear their feedback.

I later volunteered as Educational Chair of the Cambridge-Yerevan Soviet Sister City Association (1986-87) and took a class in Armenian literature. I loved reading Yeghishe Charents, but fell asleep during the small tutorials, bored by the professor's lectures.

Jon and I returned to Naples in 1988, spending time with Molly and Paolo Bazzicalupo. We had both read Carlo Levi's autobiographical novel *Christ Stopped at Eboli,* where he wrote that the people of Eboli in Southern Italy were left "outside the boundaries of progress and time." Levi inspired us to want to explore the underdeveloped "boot" region, so we drove to the Taranto region, where Greek ruins mentioned in our guidebook were still half buried in those rural areas. We found nothing to buy for supper except sandwiches. We then drove to Amalfi, where Jon became enamored with the 17th century monastery, while I vowed never to return, terrified by the miles of hairpin turns (being in the passenger side, I could see the precipitous drops). Jon later held one of his lab retreats in Amalfi.

We traveled again to Utah, this time to hike in Little Wildhorse, a slot canyon we naively tried to tackle, despite overhead storm clouds. The clouds led to a light drizzle, which became hail, and eventually torrential downpours. I turned our experience into an article (it was becoming my specialty to write about mistakes I've made and what "not do do") which was published in the *New York Times* on March 20, 1994. Here is part of the article:

> *We stride along the canyon's twisted interior. Sheets of water pour over the lip of the plateau onto our backs. I feel like I'm in a shower that is turned on full blast. A warning on our Utah map flashes through my mind: "If you get caught in a flash flood in a narrows, it will probably be fatal..."*
>
> *We thrash through pools whose water level is rising by the minute. It is now above our knees...*
>
> *We do not talk, except for an occasional yell—"Faster!", "Okay?", "Slow down!" The canyon is filling up like a glass*

under a running faucet. The water soon reaches our waists. We could swim if we must, I think...

Adrenaline and the nightmare of a flash flood drive us... I've lost my sense of time, distance and the beauty of these sandstone walls.

The light from the canyon's entrance appears, suddenly, startling us. We emerge from Little Wildhorse drenched and blinking...

Jon and I later gave a talk at the Cambridge Center for Adult Education with slides on hiking and camping in Utah.

Later that year, Jon and I took our most strenuous bike trip: we bicycled and camped in the Cele River area in France and then struggled up and over the Pyrenees. We found a campground, where Jon lay prostate for a full day. We assumed he had the flu, but it turned out to be his mitral valve prolapse condition, which was worsening. If his doctor had known of our ambitious biking plan, he would have warned him that such strenuous exercise, given his condition, was unadvisable.

Publishing

BACK HOME, my mental health was improving. That one year of therapy gave me the nerve to apply for a job co-writing a book with the president of FairTest, a non-profit whose mission was to expose the flaws in standardized tests and advocate for colleges to stop requiring them. I was told it would be a challenge to co-write with the president and it turned out to be a grueling year-long process. My co-author would dictate what he wanted to say, but when I went to straighten out repetitions or adjust the language, he'd reverse my edits. I did the whole job for about $5000. My agent negotiated for $500 extra when I was asked to do a little promotion, which I hadn't signed up to do (although I had written a small piece on the book for *Essence* magazine).

Our book, *Standing Up to the SAT: The Test-Taker's Bill of Rights* (1989), was a slim paperback, but it contained a strong critique that could empower students, parents, and other advocates. Simon & Schuster/Prentice-Hall/ARCO was a topnotch publisher, which had planned a print run of 15,000, but then upped it to 20,000. The New York Public Library named it as one of the best 1991 books for teenagers. The book's cover played up the foreword by former NOW president Eleanor Smeal and the afterword by Ralph Nader: I later wrote a wry essay about how I could hardly spot my name at all on the cover of our book.

An unexpected benefit of this book project was that, in order to critique biases in the math as well as English sections, I had to relearn algebra and geometry and so I was able to recover some of my math ability while researching for the book. But during the long process of writing the book, my body suffered. I got both a case of repetitive strain injury, and a painful case of stress-induced shingles.

After my co-writing job, I was hired by Educators for Social Responsibility to write *Communism and Anti-Communism: Voices From History,* a teaching module for high schools. This is the description that appeared in their catalog, announcing the upcoming book:

> *The 10-week curriculum explores communism and anticommunism in the United States. Through first-person accounts, trial transcripts, communist and anticommunist tracts, and class exercises, students look through the eyes of Communists, anticommunists, communist exiles and people blacklisted as communists.*
>
> *Students look at the historical consequences of periods of communist activities and repression.*

> *The focus of* Communism and Anti-Communism *is on balancing individual freedom and national security.*

I felt strongly that I couldn't write about anti-communism unless it included a multi-faceted view of communism (the good and the bad). The historian who reviewed my draft didn't like that approach and gave me extensive rewrites. Just as that was happening, the USSR fell apart and the Cold War ended. So, although ESR had put the title in their catalogue, they said it wasn't relevant anymore, and they never published it.

In retrospect, I realized that the topic was so densely historical *and* politically polarizing that the project was probably out of my league.

More than solo projects, I've always loved projects that are joint efforts. Every other year, I worked to compile and publish a "family book" about some subject that family members could contribute to:

- *Tell Me an Old Old Story* collected stories from various family members.
- *The Smart and Silly Book* was filled with clever and amusing things that members of the Shutt Family said as kids—four generations.
- *Our Ordinary Days* collected what a typical "good day" was for various relatives (I interviewed many over the phone for the first edition) so that we could picture them wherever they lived.
- *Family Music* - was a tape recording of music or singing by various members of the family, including a cut from an old record of Mom, Dad, Bibsy and Stevie singing.
- *Dad's 80th birthday booklet* included Dad and Mom's writings and advocacy letters by all of us.

Memories of a Small-town Boy was a very personal project that I took on: to record, type out, edit and print a booklet of my father's oral stories about growing up in Boalsburg, Pennsylvania. His second wife Dottie made me take out all the swear words ("god-damn," "hell of a," "Christ Almighty"), which took away some, but not all, of the earthy flavor of his stories. As we worked together on the stories, for the first time Dad and I were "buddies": I played "business manager" and he was the star. In 1990, we traveled together to Boalsburg and sold his "book" at stores in that town. I did a second booklet on his work life, and a third on his activism.

Given those projects, it seemed "right up my alley" (collaborating with friends *and* getting paid) when my friends Charlie Holley, Susan Porter, and J. Curtis Jones hired me to co-write, with their Tribal Rhythms team, an article for *Harvard Educational Review*. The racially diverse group had been working for 20 years to integrate the arts into urban and suburban schools via participatory music and theater. Satisfying Harvard's demand for revisions was a grueling but rewarding experience.

The following year, I wrote a book proposal for Tribal Rhythms (their agent failed to find an interested publisher, so they self-published it on their own). I was also freelancing for the local paper *The Tab*, *Nuclear Times*, *The Boston Globe*, and other publications. But I seemed to still be looking for what I thought of as "a real job." I got help with my resume at the Women's Industrial and Educational Union in Boston (years later, Ben did the same) and the Cambridge Job Counseling Center.

To See Words Again

I FOUND my second adjunct professor job in 1988, teaching journalism at Suffolk University, a subway ride from home. I wanted students to learn about freelancing not through a textbook (which I did require but mostly ignored), but by finding a topic they considered important, and then reporting *and* rewriting until their work was good enough to submit for publication. They appreciated me giving them a real (if challenging) journalism/freelance experience.

I then shifted to an adjunct job in Emerson College's journalism department to teach magazine writing. It was a great experience, especially since several students got their articles published, and at least one, Kira Salak, went on to write for *National Geographic* and then author three books that were all well-received.

Although I loved the courses I was teaching, I started to feel that it didn't allow me time for my own writing. I also needed to organize another National Writers Union conference in the Spring, and to be available to Jon, who was scheduled to have heart valve surgery. I told the director that I was resigning. I wrote in my journal that "I need to see words again—my own. I've pondered my students' writing but not relished my own."

Soon, along with writing, my union activism was growing. Every other year I took the lead, working with others, on our National Writers Union "For Love and Money" writers conferences (my "executive functioning" must have been at its peak in my 40s and 50s). They drew up to 500 writers and took place at the Harvard Kennedy School of Government. I insisted that 30 percent of our speakers be gay or lesbian or people of color (that was back when quotas were okay). I organized five of these conferences, but no one was willing to take it over after that.

I set up display tables and/or spoke at OutWrite writers conferences in Boston: one speaker called me an "honorary lesbian" because of my commitment to issues facing gay and lesbian writers. I traveled to various cities for national board meetings, diversity retreats, and annual delegates assemblies. Yet I resisted being co-chair of the National Diversity Committee, wanting to follow the leadership of people of color. I ended up in that position anyway, as one of the few activists who would "hang in there" despite tensions that the issues we raised caused. Those tensions interested and challenged me, one of the reasons I later co-facilitated the course *White People Challenging Racism.*

I worked on, and we published the NWU chapter's *Insiders Guide to Freelancing in New England.* It was based on the work of the Journalism Committee and was the kind of collaborative work that I love. Later, we published *From Idea to Article,* another collaborative work.

I knew by now that showing up to places where writers of color met on their own terms was as important as inviting them to union events. So I attended Darryl Alladice's poetry series at Dorchester's Codman Square Library, and Phil Robinson's workshops at the Central Square Library, and the Dark Room Collective weekly readings, also in Central Square.

During the 1990s, I was able to publish in well-known national magazines and newspapers: *The New York Times, Essence, US Air, New Age, Smithsonian, Yoga Journal, Harvard Educational Review, Town & Gown,* and *Reminiscence.* I wrote four articles with Jon including "The Peddling Gourmets" and "From Goya to Gastronomy: Nine Small Museums of Southwest France." We gave a slide presentation at the Cambridge Center for Adult Education on our gourmet bicycling article, with tips on how to plan routes, how to backpack, and best times to travel. Our experience was unusual because most people who bicycle in France do it with a tour and a guide and hotels all lined up. We *liked* to bike with the uncertainty of finding a campground that night.

However, many topics I researched and pitched to national magazines did *not* result in an assignment ("what to do when your friend freaks out," "decluttering," "sexual sculptures on Romanesque churches," etc.). That's par for the course, but I got frustrated. My brother-in-law Peter Salmon sent me supportive letters, the kind my mother would have written, and they were important to me. He was also freelancing as an artist, making sporadic, not steady, sales, and shared how he felt helped by therapy:

> *It helped me feel sure about what I already knew—when I can be completely engaged in my work, I take its value for granted. The despair sets in when I wonder about its value instead of doing it.*

He compared his father's newspaper career, working six days a week and 50 weeks a year, to the lifestyle Jon and I led, with the "rhythm of the academic year" that gave us "time for walking down canyons, checking out wildflowers and other important personal joys."

> *Although you feel the loneliness of this kind [freelance] of journalism, you also see the potential for real thought development and human communication in writing features.*

> *It seems to me that you can have your cake and eat it too—the adventurous life you and Jon live—writing about things that matter to you, by accepting some of the admitted agonies of the freelance life.*

I was given a PEN New England "Friend to Writers" annual award in 1991, the only award (aside from my "best sport" high school award) I've ever received:

> *"Beckwith, a journalist and book author, has been the heart and soul of the NWUBoston Local since 1984. She produces a monthly newsletter, organized the last three biennial writers' conferences at the Kennedy School, serves as a conduit between needy writers and sources of help and information, and tirelessly promotes the union and urges writers to stand up on their hind legs and demand what they are due.*

The Boston Local, now very active, with over 700 members, would scarcely exist without her persistence."

I accepted it with some chagrin: it was about me as an activist, not as a writer. But also, I've often struggled with praise like this. Perhaps it is some kind of insecurity that doesn't allow me to accept someone's fulsome compliments. Or is it my honest self-evaluation coming up against what I see as an exaggerated assessment of myself? Perhaps it traces back to my mother's admonition to "accept everyone — except snobbish people" that echoes in my head and prevents me from accepting plaudits too quickly.

Travel Writing

We visited France again in 1992, traveling now by car, to museums in hilly Southwest France to co-write an article published in *The Washington Post.* We visited our friends Josette Rouvier and Nesh Yaniv at their home in Mende-Les-Causse on Bastille Day. They led us on an hours-long walk, ending in an hours-long feast where the guests took turns reading Montaigne's—in Old French.

Our outdoors experiences were starting to get more interesting. While in Utah in 1992, after a precipitous Fishers Towers hike with my cousin Betsey, we visited the Bookers. Bob Booker was a ranger who told us where to find rock art (Dirty Devil, Rochester Creek). We stumbled upon an *American Rock Art Research Association* conference focused on protecting the art and then visited rock art sites that Dr. Dorman told us about. We realized that these dedicated activists would tell us about such sites only after we'd earned their trust.

The following year, we visited Utah and Arizona, spending time in Tuba City, where our friend Dan Levy was serving as a doctor in its tribal hospital. We bought lunch at a local indigenous fair and ate with native people who bought lunches, then ate together—without talking, a new experience for us, but a cultural norm.

We hiked along Utah's Comb Ridge, an 80-mile sandstone "monocline" that's shaped like a rooster's comb. We crept up to the ridge's edge and peered over, then quickly backed away. The sight of the 1,000 foot drop gave us vertigo. Later, looking over a lesser cliff edge, we spotted a panel of pictographs and petroglyphs that we hadn't known about. We loved the pictograph and petroglyph images because no one knows what they mean, leaving us free to guess and wonder.

In 1994, we took a trip to France: La Rochelle Oradour and Chambon. We were researching and writing about World War II resistance museums—and we were impressed to find that the Huguenot tradition of activism on behalf of oppressed people continued. I interviewed museum workers for that article—in French. We co-wrote a long article, but it never got published.

1995 saw us hiking in Utah to research and write an article on seeking out Indian rock art for the *Washington Post.* I also interviewed art restorer Constance Silver who worked to clear off twentieth century graffiti from the Anasazi rock art panel at Buckskin Gulch for another article, which I unsuccessfully pitched to *Smithsonian* magazine.

~

Back home, I somehow developed rotator cuff tendinitis: I couldn't lift my arms high to reach for things. I did physical therapy and at-home exercises for months before I finally regained my strength and mobility. From then on, I decided I would need to be a "student of my body" in order to not let body part breakdowns keep me from playing sports.

Anthony married Cori in 1994, and in 1995 Cori gave birth to Daniel, our first grandson. I babysat for him in Jamaica Plain and then at their River Street house in Arlington: a special treat, but a big responsibility.

Cori gave birth to Adam in 1996. I would pick up both boys up from their babysitter and stay with them until Cori got home from work. Later, I picked Daniel up from his pre-school. The teachers there heard him call out to me "Hi, Barbara!" and told him to call me by my proper title: Grandma.

When the kids came to my house, I tried to write down (just like my mother did when her three girls were young) every funny or smart thing they said:

Daniel's questions at different times:

Why is water floatable?

Why do trees grow?

Why do people need eyes?

If you keep going in space and get to the end, what's on the other side?

How come you can "do nothing" since everything has a name for what you do?

What if I had 20 brothers and an infinity of sisters? That would be the same as infinity, right?

Adam said, as we drove through Central Square: *There are lots of different kinds of people in our country.*

He tells Jon*: I like friends. But I don't like dead friends.*

At Franklin Park Zoo, Adam exclaimed: *When we go to see the butterflies, we'll FLING the door open and the butterflies will be all around!* (impressive that he used the verb fling)

WHILE IN MY 60s, I found that squash continued to feed my physical and social passions. I played on the Mt. Auburn Club women's "C League" team, which won the 1996-1997 inter-club championship. For a year, I offered a free 45-minute introduction to the sport. I taught dozens of people the game and helped them find players at their level. I also swam and took stretch and strengthening classes. I wrote to my father about a 1995 competition with Tufts University's squash team:

I was the big surprise of the competition. No one, I guess, expects someone my age to beat a woman in her 20s, and another who runs marathons and triathlons.

The club squash coach, Mohammed, reminded me to "play smart" (my drive isn't strong but my placement is clever). I lost my final match, but thought about the joy in "giving it my best shot." And I remembered your story about the Olympic wrestling tryouts and how they'd run you ragged the days before.

I had dug up our garden the day before my match, which I showed up for on time, warmed myself up, then was told my match had been switched and would be two hours later. But I had agreed to staff a union table at a book fair after my scheduled match! So I had to bike back home, load up books, race down to Harvard Square and set up the table, frantically calling members to get a sub, and then race back to the gym in time for my match.

So yes, I lost, but I took it in stride, knowing that I "gave it my best shot."

But my eight-year struggle with plantar fasciitis started around that time, probably exacerbated by playing squash. I went to a variety of medical and sports professionals and tried every cure: exercises, ice, nighttime "boots," pain killers, shots, stretches, different shoes. In 1998 I wrote a "foot journal" every day for 6 months, writing down what I did and what caused pain or relief.

The Mount Auburn Club decided to close its squash courts, but a group of us fought that closing (they'd been falsely advertising that squash would still be available). I ended up joining the Boston Sports Club for awhile. I wrote to my sister that I'd lost 15 pounds playing squash: my doctor became alarmed and told me not to lose any more, so half of those lost pounds slowly returned. In 2020, the Mt. Auburn club was finally torn down—a huge life science research center now sits on the site. Despite the setback, I joined the Concord Acton Squash Club (now "Squashwest") where I regularly played up to five times a week with Hilary Yates and other women players until 2023.

~

In the 1990s, I continued to publish, but wanted to write longer articles that would dive deeper into social and racial issues that I cared about.

In 1997, I took a semester-long Boston University narrative journalism seminar (Mark Kramer's "Writing About Society") that allowed me to research and write "immersion" articles. To ensure that each of us would get peer support as well as instructor criticism, I organized my fellow students into a mutual feedback system. Two articles that I wrote in this seminar—a profile of Carrie Dearborn (a wheelchair user trying to become a comedian) and "Tournament Tough" (about a woman competing in the national women's squash tournament for the first time)—were published in both magazines and anthologies.

My confidence as a writer increased. I imagined that I could write a book, and wrote a proposal with a working title of "Swap Talk: Tales of People Making Change." It would be be grounded in oral history-type storytelling by grassroots activists in Mothers Against Drunk Driving, Grey Panthers, the union "9-5", the Black Women's Health Project, CASA, the American-Arab Anti-Discrimination League, the Coalition Against Handguns, Greenpeace, the Boston Area Gay and Lesbian Youth, Rosie's Place, ACT UP, Save Our Schools (Chicago), and Educators for Social Responsibility.

My proposal read, in part:

Who will read Swap Talk? People who want change of some sort: from curbing drunk driving, to funding AIDS research, to

> *getting drug dealers out of the neighborhood, to recycling, to housing the homeless, to starting a workplace union, to stopping racism or homophobia, to gaining wheelchair accessibility, to getting smaller classes in neighborhood schools.*
>
> *Swap Talk will give the reader an idea of how to organize, not through "how to" instructions that books on organizing tend to use, but through stories of real groups and their real struggles.*

Around this time, I was attending community organizing meetings led by Michael Brown, a professional organizer with 20 years experience. He was also writing a book proposal, and it was on the same topic. He wanted my feedback on his proposal, so we swapped proposals. I could see that he had a similar idea, and also had much more experience as a paid community organizer than I. So in the end, I abandoned my proposal—although in retrospect, it would have explored organizing in a different and valuable way and I should have had the confidence to pursue it.

SINCE THE 1980s, Jon and I had been taking "reading weekends" (no sight-seeing, just reading, short walks, and eating well) in quiet places, like seaside Ogunquit, in Maine. We found the weekend to be a way to fully immerse ourselves in a few good books, so we continued these getaways about twice a year, for more than 20 years. I wrote a personal essay about our experience, which I submitted to the *New York Times*. The *Times* published it in 1993, proving that while my topic may have seemed ordinary (after all, everyone reads on a weekend getaway), the *way* I wrote it was not.

In 1999, we traveled again to Utah to take part in a documentation project for the Southwest Utah Wilderness Association. We were assigned a section of wilderness area, taking pictures to show that a claimed "road" was actually just a faint trail, worthy of wilderness protection.

We also traveled to Amalfi, Italy, this time overland, where Jon's lab reunion conference took place. I wandered around the hilltop town, at one point helping a woman lug heavy bags of groceries up steep steps, as she complained that her son wouldn't help. She insisted that I come into her home and have Limoncello, the traditional Italian drink, which caused an embarrassingly deep pink full-body flush.

~

Playing squash

Speaking at a writers' event

My grandsons Daniel and Adam enjoying a good laugh

9
MOVING FROM TALK TO ACTION

I had been working for years on diversity issues with people of color and white allies in the National Writers Union. But I needed a place to think through various controversial issues so that I could focus on the work from a knowledgeable point of view, while staying open and sensitive to a range of perspectives. In 2000, I saw that the Cambridge Center for Adult Education offered me such a place, through their *White People Challenging Racism: Moving from Talk to Action* (WPCR) workshop, led by Jennifer Yanco.

I took the workshop and felt challenged, but was willing to reflect on my own upbringing. I'd been raised in isolated 1940s and 1950s suburban cultures. At the same time that civil rights activism and women's liberation were on the rise in the 1960s, I started to live in cities and got to know a wider range of people, just as civil rights and gender equality movements were emerging. My class and racial awareness increased: in reflecting on my 1950s upbringing, I began to see how racial exclusion had given me unearned advantages. I wrote and shared a frank essay: *Growing Up Oblivious*:

My family moved a lot when I was young, choosing towns for their "good schools." Those schools always turned out to be overrated; the "good school" mantra I now realize was mostly code for "white and Protestant." I remember thinking of the few Catholics in town as exotic -- and therefore suspect.

During my elementary school years, we lived in Garden City, a Long Island suburb that The New York Times recently reported had kept assessments of older homes at 1950s levels. Newer residents -- Jewish, Black, and Hispanic families who came in after we moved away -- had been paying unfairly higher taxes, effectively underwriting the older parts of town...

In college, my class of 500 had just two African American students: Amalya Kearse, who became a New York Superior judge, and Shirlee Taylor Haizlip, the author of The Sweeter the Berry, a memoir about discovering why her mother seemed sad and lonely: a branch of their light-skinned family had faced so much job discrimination that they moved far away and lived as white. I had never before considered that those of us who see ourselves as white may be more colorful than we think.

Jennifer and I joined a small group of women writers who felt compelled to express, in poetry and prose, their deep dismay at the racially unjust systems we're part of. I shared my *Growing Up Oblivious* essay at a reading we gave at a Martin Luther King Jr. service in Boston. I was later invited by Bernestine Singley to read my essay at events celebrating her book *When Race Becomes Real: Black and White Writers Confront Their Personal Histories*.

After taking the WPRC workshop a second time, I was ready to commit myself to concrete action in every sphere of my life. Eventually, I moved from student to facilitator, when Jennifer asked me to co-lead the workshop with her. Other participants became co-facilitators, and the workshop was offered in other venues, including Wellesley College. The workshop continues today (in person and via Zoom) and we now have a more racially diverse facilitator group, led by Black women.

My presenter bio from a White Privilege conference described more about my upbringing:

> *I'd been raised in racially isolated suburbs that had been regulated, by law and commercial practices, to ensure that they [the residents] were all white. I had no teachers of color in K-12 nor in my New England college, where racial inequity was assumed to be caused by "the culture of poverty" (as Black Southerners were risking their livelihoods – and lives – to get access to libraries, schools, stores, buses and ballot boxes).*
>
> *I'd earned two graduate degrees, co-led various "diversity" efforts, considered myself a progressive feminist, and could recognize subtle dynamics of institutionalized sexism. But only after living in cities where I got to know a wider range of people, and now by taking WPCR could I see the depth and breadth of my country's institutionalized racial inequity and take seriously my responsibility to help dismantle it.*

When I learned that the 25-year-old anti-racist organization Community Change Inc. (CCI) was the fiscal sponsor of the WPCR workshops, I immediately joined and became a volunteer at CCI's library committee, carrying on the work of Yvonne Pappenheim. She had built CCI's *Library on Racism*, the only library in the country with a focus on racism, white privilege, and the history of struggles for racial justice. We entered all of the books into the computer system and put labels on each of its 2,500 books (now housed at Northeastern University). I also volunteered for CCI's Drylongso Awards Committee that annually awards "ordinary people doing extraordinary work against racism," and reviewed and recommended racism-related books for the Gustavus Meyers book awards.

Others in my family were similarly concerned. My sister Joanne, an art teacher concerned about her students' prejudices, took a week-long Community Wide Dialogue to End Racism course offered by the InterReligious Council of Central NY, in Syracuse, near were she lived. My sister Linda and her husband Peter organized a civil rights conference in 2004, hosted by their Episcopal church in the Poconos. The 2-day event, *50 Years of Civil Rights: How Far Have We Come, How Far We Have to Go*, drew a diverse group of people who shared experiences, listened to each others' concerns, and committed themselves to advancing racial equity in the area ("Kill NYers" graffiti was showing up as the area's demographics were changing, bringing racial diversity to its formerly white population). Trinity Church is now the most fully integrated Episcopal Church in their county.

THE TERRORIST ATTACKS on September 11, 2001, shocked the country. It also drove me to do something useful, positive, and collaborative. I wrote at the time: "I have purged my sadness & anger over the terrorist attack by doing something that will make the world better."

All that year, I threw myself into our NWU diversity committee's ambitious and multi-faceted project: the compilation of a 100-page guide called *Strength Through Diversity: A Handbook for Locals* (100 writers contributed to it). It's a great document, but since it was largely available only as a pdf from the union's website, activists were reluctant to download it (they weren't yet "ready" for that medium and internet speeds were not what they are today). It probably rarely got used, even though its insights remain relevant today.

That same year, Jon spent his mornings writing his memoir *Making Genes, Making Waves: A Social Activist in Science.* His writing was elegant and accessible. I gave him some "writing for everyday people" advice (use straightforward sentences, strong action verbs, fewer adjectives). But it was his honesty, his humility, and especially his quirky stories that made his narrative unique. Few scientists would think to start their memoir chapters with French quail farmers, movie lines, characters from Utah, or flowers flying through lab windows. It was published in 2002 by Harvard University Press (our friends Ed Hart and Anita Robboy hosted his book party lunch), but wasn't reprinted as a paperback (it is available as an eBook today).

Also that year, Jon and I took a trip to Argentina. After his science conference was over, we traveled to the Northwest part of the country, into the desert, with high altitude mountains and indigenous communities. Remembering Jon's heart doctor's warnings, we quickly returned to low altitude cities after visiting high altitude villages. As usual, I readily understood what Argentinians said, but once I translated for Jon, he was able to respond in Spanish with a better accent than mine.

After several years of foot pain that was making hiking and squash—and even walking—difficult, I went to Peter Stone, who specialized in sports injuries and had worked with Olympians and professional athletes. After my problems cleared up, I wrote a wry essay, "Adventures in Self-Cure" for *New Age* magazine (its "Body and Soul" issue). I also pressed Stone to add images of women athletes to the waiting room poster display, which at the time was only of males.

But another body problem appeared. I went to the doctor about a sore above my lip that wasn't going away, only to discover that it was basal cell cancer. I had surgery to remove the cancer, spending the day waiting as they examined each layer they'd removed, bringing me back four times for removal of another layer. I wrote another wry essay for WBUR's commentary project *Cognoscenti* called "Losing my Philtrum," (the vertical groove between your nose and your upper lip), in part to cope with the ordeal by making an amusing story out of the experience. I was again turning my experiences into writing as a way to cope and process events—often through humor. I think this is why I like people who make me laugh: it's a certain perspective on life that isn't "moaning and groaning", but taking a humorous approach to whatever life may throw at you.

~

My father, Joe Shutt, died on August 24, 2004, of an apparent stroke while recovering from a fall and broken hip. He was healthy most of his life and lived 98 years with all his hair, all his teeth, and all his wits and graciousness intact. We'd had good times together doing oral history projects (starring Dad) and in the last two years I had driven out to Pennsylvania often to see him.

He spent his last day in a nursing home, but his mind remained clear: he went in his wheelchair to vote, and when an election official inappropriately told him how much money was being proposed for the infrastructure referendum, he replied "bridges and roads?" and voted yes, to her shock. I later wrote the election commission with a complaint about the poll worker trying to influence his vote. My sisters Joanne and Linda were with him when he died. We later held a joyous memorial outdoors outside our Henryville house, with people telling stories, Joe Shutt-style.

It's possible that my father's "problem-solver" instincts and his later political activism had an impact on my years of involvement in many social and political issues that I found important. In the late 1980s, I wrote a letter to my father, expressing my appreciation for him and his impact on me:

Dear Dad,

I'm a do-er because all my life I've watched you be an action kind of guy. I don't give up when I believe in something because I've watched you stick to it all your life...I get my persistence in [actions like] shaping a union for writers from you because your skill is remarkable in this area.

During World War II, my father had been hired by Sperry Gyroscope and the U.S. War Department New York to boost the domestic workforce. At the direction of his bosses, he aggressively recruited women, African Americans, and people with disabilities (who previously had not been target demographics), hiring 3000 workers within a few months. In part due to his efforts, Sperry received a national award from the NAACP for advancing the economic opportunity of African Americans.

Starting in his late 60s, Dad was heavily involved in Common Cause, a government accountability organization. His main concern was gun control and he became their Florida membership chairman, then a district head, and finally the president of the Florida branch. The Palm Beach Post wrote in 1979 that: "[Joe Shutt] lectures on money power vs. people power in government." From 1976 to 1995, my father was featured in Florida newspapers at least 288 times, mostly related to gun control.

Dad had been an NRA member, having grown up with rifles. But when Joe was just eleven years old, he had almost taken his life with a handgun after learning about his father's sudden death, and the memory of that moment motivated his gun control activism in his later life. His second wife, Dottie, had witnessed a young boy shoot himself in the head when she was only ten years old (the boy didn't know the gun was loaded) and so also harbored a life-long concern about firearms and firearm safety. For close to 25 years, dad organized, gave talks, and debated gun control issues with "the other side" on radio and local television shows.

THE YEAR 2005 brought fresh body challenges: Jon had a bicycle accident on the Boston University bridge on his way to the lab. He was found passed out on the end of the bridge. He had a broken shoulder and a hematoma on his brain, but he recovered. I got my first "replacement part"—a cataract operation (the other eye was done about a year later). I once again turned to essay-writing to process my experience, writing "Recovering My Blues," the title referring to the fact that I had been losing my ability to see the color blue. (The essay was published on WBUR's *Cognoscenti* site.)

I turned 70 in 2007 and decided to compete again in the national women's amateur squash tournament at Harvard. I was the oldest; the youngest was 14. My opponents were in their 30s and 40s. I won two of my four games, which felt pretty good. Jon saw me play squash for the first time and thought I was losing because I hit to the four corners—he assumed I should be hitting to the center and he didn't understand the scoring system.

CHARLES COE AND I, as long-term co-chairs, kept the Boston Chapter of the NWU on an even keel. Charles and I made sure that our chapter's voice was heard on local issues. I spoke out at the State House to ensure that Boston's new downtown Literary District would recognize Boston's vibrant 19th century Black literary community. At Charles' urging, I also pressed the Boston Globe to support the proposed Massachusetts Poet Laureate and to press for a stipend, since whoever was chosen would be expected to travel to all corners of the state and shouldn't be forced to pay expenses out of pocket.

I gave several National Writers Union talks and workshops, finally getting comfortable with myself as an "expert" on topics like "The Art of Communicating with Editors." I gave talks at the New Hampshire Writers Day "Writing for Love and Money" panel, the Women Action & Media conference ("How to Get Heard: The Art of Strategic Communication with Editors workshop"), and the Boston University College of Communication Graduate seminar ("Marketing Your Articles").

At this point, I was meeting monthly with my essay group and weekly with my writing buddy Susan, but I was submitting less—and when I did submit, publishing less. I was largely back to where I started: writing as my way to think, feel, and act.

I share that *need* to write with my sister Joanne. For several years, she's been journaling daily, capturing sounds, tastes, touches, smells, tidbits of conversations, and small anecdotes of our shared lives that I wouldn't otherwise recall. How each of us writes is "WYSIWG": what you see is what you get.

My life at this time was divided into equally satisfying parts: squash (playing five times a week), teaching (essay writing and co-facilitating White People Challenging Racism), organizing (National Writers Union), family and friends, and writing.

I was following our family motto: "No regrets."

~

Hiking in Utah, 1980s, where we actually did sink into quicksand

National Writers Union Diversity Retreat, Minneapolis, 2005

10
COMMUNITY

Back in 1967, when we moved from a cramped apartment three blocks from Harvard Square to a short leafy dead-end street a mile from the Square, I was upset: I thought we were moving too far from "the action." But I was wrong. The community of neighbors turned out to be important and enriching to our lives.

Between Appleton Road and neighboring Appleton Street, there were six 2-family homes, with 12 families that interacted daily. Our kids, along with kids from neighboring streets, gathered after school, a gang of public, private, and Catholic school kids, playing on our mostly traffic-free road: kicking soccer balls, twirling hula hoops, throwing frisbees, learning to ride bikes or perfecting a skateboard move, drawing chalk fantasies, and talking, joking or arguing, unheard by us adults.

We each had a side yard that could be a driveway: a landscaper assumed that we and the Bartons next door would want a hedge separating our properties. But, inspired by our 1960s values, we both decided to instead create a terrace where neighbors could gather. A friend offered to do the work, but laid down friable "inside bricks" that quickly crumbled. We replaced them with sturdy "outside bricks" that are still holding together today.

The gathering space was soon dubbed "Red Square". Yes, the bricks were red, but we weren't Communists, just committed leftists: on that "people's patio," Jim would host Cambridge Tenants Organizing Committee meetings; in the 1970s, our Harvard graduate student neighbor met with African anti-Apartheid activists to organize divestment protests; in our apartment, we hosted strategy meetings on writers' rights, nuclear arms protests and genetics and society issues.

Over the years, some who rented would eventually buy. Others moved away but stayed in touch. Different neighbors hosted a variety of community gatherings: mint juleps on Kentucky Derby day, New Year's "ball drops," yoga workouts, garlic potlucks, scotch tastings, HONK practice, hot tub dips, open readings, kids' fairs and yard sales, barbecues, and picnics on the terrace.

The "Beckwith Dance Parties" were also a regular feature of the neighborhood. We held 51 of them, starting in the 1970s. We'd first been drawn into "the dance circuit" by our friends Nathalie Merchant, Anne Monticone, and A.E. Ryan, crashing parties around town that Nathalie would get wind of, and frequenting Boston's Lansdowne Street clubs.

Eventually Jon and I started to host our own, open to anyone who wanted to dance. Jon spent hours selecting music from his vinyl collection and later as 90-minute cassettes (a new one for each party). He'd ask teenaged Anthony "what's the latest?" to keep his line-up fresh. One 1980s cassette bounced from Diana Ross to Sheena Easton, Dolly Parton, Stevie Wonder, the Stranglers, The Blues Project, Donna Summer, George Benson, back to Stevie Wonder, then Otis Redding and back to George Benson, Blondie, the B-52s, Queenie, and Heart. In later decades, Jon would include salsa, house, world, funk, techno, fados, and tango music to keep the dance floor filled.

The mix of people was invigorating: Jon's new post-docs who had heard our parties were not to be missed, old friends, my younger squash partners, neighbors of different ages, activist friends. We'd serve a powerful punch to loosen things up (we watered it down in later years). The parties would draw 75 to 100 people over the course of the night.

The dance floor would become packed with gyrating couples, groups, or solo freestyle dancers. Dancers would work up a sweat, open windows to gulp fresh air, or move to the side room where we'd set up a projector with slides for the dancers who needed a break, or non-dancers who liked to talk. The slides displayed cacti flowers, erotic Romanesque church sculpture, ancient rock art, and hiking/biking scenes, which were all good topics for conversation.

Cigarette smokers hung out on our front porch; those who brought pot could gather in the attic room. At midnight, we'd serve black beans to bolster the dancers. Around 1 a.m., we'd close the windows and gradually turn down the music, to respect neighbors trying to sleep—and to avoid a "Quiet down!" visit from the Cambridge police. We'd eventually take off our "come on in; no need to knock" sign from our front door, clear out the attic and porch, get a friend to drive home who had over-indulged. Jon and I would do one last slow dance, then cut off the music. Our "dance circuit" friends would stay till 2 a.m., if necessary, to help clean up the place, after which Jon and I would head for bed, épuisé.

WHEN WE LIVED IN PARIS, we were attracted by French culture, particularly how friends gathered regularly at neighborhood cafés. We and other American expatriates hung out at the Café de Seine, drinking coffee, having long conversations at sidewalk tables, watching people walking by as they watched us. Inspired by this experiences, Jon and I started, in the 1990s, emailing friends: "We're meeting for drinks after work at 5 p.m. Join us!" We'd walk to Harvard Square and settle in at a bar. In good weather, we'd meet at one of the area's outdoor plazas, pulling up tables and chairs for the few or many friends who would show up.

Monied friends would order a cocktail and an overpriced snack; less-monied friends could get by with coffee or a soft drink. These casual drop-ins were our way of keeping in touch with disparate friends, who soon became friends with each other. Instead of talking about work, they'd share passions: bicycling, Iranian movies, film noir, music, food, politics (here and abroad), and language (Italian, Turkish, French). The gatherings continued for two decades.

When we reached our 70s, we shifted our party hosting to afternoon get-togethers: twice a year "drinks, eats and conversation."

Jon and I loved to go to Cambridge parties

11
LE MISTRAL

My writing in the last 15 years has increasingly focused on racism: revealing my ignorance, ah-ha moments, mistakes, and my action-taking, hoping to inspire other white people to do the same. I self-published three personal essay booklets (formatted by my squash partner, Hilary Yates) over the next few years, titled *What Was I Thinking?* with subtitles *Reflecting on Everyday Racism* (2009), *Digging Deeper into Everyday Racism* (2013), and *Questions and Quandaries* (2015). I handed them out at White People Challenging Racism workshops that I was co-facilitating.

At a White Privilege conference, I stopped at the table of Crandall, Dostie and Douglass Books and proposed to publisher Jeff Hitchcock that my inexpensive booklets would be good introductions leading to his hardback book offerings. He agreed to distribute my booklets, which were then sold for years on cddbooks.com.

I also contributed two essays to the White Privilege Conference Journal, "Reconciled to Jargon" (2013), and "In the Face of Resistance—A Lay Facilitator's Experience" (2014), but I struggled with the online editing process, never having learned some of the new technologies, like Dropbox. I also contributed "Aha

Moments" to the *2LeafPress* 2016 anthology *What Does It Mean to be White in America?*

My friendships from several decades converged in the mid-2010s. I'd known Elena Dodd Harap from college in the 1950s and had recently connected with her through racial justice activism. She'd created a Women's Writing Workshop for older women (50s to 80s) living in Jamaica Plain, Roxbury and Dorchester, in the belief that "women often lack a space in which their inner thoughts are welcomed and encouraged." She asked me to coach the workshop (her family in California needed her); and next year, to co-coach with her.

When I needed help with the grant that allowed the workshop to be offered for free, I reconnected with Steve Chase, a former 1970s Home Base student of mine. He had become a Mission-Hill-Fenway Neighborhood Trust board member and was able to help me with the application process.

I was delighted that Loretta Dixon was a workshop participant (we'd been anti-racism library volunteers together), allowing us to renew our friendship via writing.

When we hired Hilary Yates to produce our essay anthology, I appreciated her not only as my friend and squash partner, but as a graphic artist.

Over the 10-session workshop, the women wrote creative, thought-provoking, personal essays with titles like "Concept of Self," "The Power of a Name," "Chosing Grey Hair," "Jews are Used to Walls," "Dios de Los Muertos," "I Love Roxbury." As a coach for the workshop, I learned as much as I mentored.

It was a wonderful experience, having separate strands of my life braided together for this single project.

BETWEEN 2008 AND 2020, I found myself doing a lot of speaking events at a variety of venues. These appealed to my extrovert self, and my desire to engage people personally on issues I cared about. I was part of lecture series, panels, and workshops, including a Cambridge Center for Adult Education *Morning Lecture Series* on speaking up against racism; delivering the talk *Racism: Addressing the White Problem*; being on a Cambridge School of Weston panel on *Being an Ally*; and a workshop on teaching anti-racism at the *Race and Pedagogy National Conference* at Puget Sound University.

I also finally found a "home" for the wry personal essays that feel the most like "me." The radio station WBUR launched *Cognoscenti*, its online "commentary" series, whose editors wanted my essays about racism, body issues, and family-related topics, and brought me into their recording studio to tape two of them. *Cognoscenti* asked me to do a weekly column relating to aging, but I declined (I didn't want the pressure of producing essays weekly). I found the short essay format a perfect fit for my way of thinking and writing style and they published nine of my essays (from 2014-2016), which are still available on their website:

- *You Don't Know What You've Got Till It's Gone*
- *The Age of Innocence: When I Didn't Know What I Didn't Know About Sex*
- *Getting Warmer: When Menopause Came for Me*
- *Is Racism Too Entrenched To Be Defeated?*
- *What's Behind the Power of a Stare?*
- *It's My Job, Not His, To Counter Anti-Semitic Stereotypes*
- *Toys Will be Toys: The Trouble With Toy Guns*
- *The Stories We Tell Ourselves About the People Who Came Before Us*

From 2005 to 2013, I also did more public readings of essays, which I'd learned from Charles Coe how to perform with dramatic verve. It was gratifying to hear audience members laughing, murmuring, and "getting" what I was trying to convey. In 2006, I did readings (three with Judah Leblanc) at Bestseller's Café bookstore in Medford, Squawk Coffeehouse in Cambridge,

McIntyre & Moore Booksellers in Somerville, the Cambridge Center for Adult Education, and at the Cambridge Science Festival.

Jon and I took canyon hiking trips to Utah in 2009, 2013, and 2014. During a trip to France in 2009, Jon collapsed in his soup at a restaurant and was hospitalized for three days for what turned out to be only walking pneumonia. Jon was happy that he was able to converse with hospital staff in French, as I did in the town of Apt, where the hotelier wanted constant updates on Jon, offering help as I tried to cope (buying cellphones, figuring out how to send emails).

In 2010, Jon gave another talk in France, giving us a chance for another bicycle trip—this time to Isle de Noirmoutier (west of Nantes and accessible by bridge) to see the beach where our favorite French filmmaker, Anges Varda, had filmed her documentary about widows.

Five years later, I reluctantly agreed to take one final bike trip in France to celebrate Jon's 80th birthday—I wasn't sure we could handle it at this age. We bicycled for five days in the hilly Vaucluse area in the South, including the town of Banon, where there was a sprawling, but charming, bookstore. Despite being in "the middle of nowhere," the store was a *vaux le voyage* ("worth the trip") destination for book lovers. On the way back, we fought the fierce "Le Mistral" wind as French bicyclists biking *with* the wind called out "Turn around! You're going in the wrong direction!" Of course, I wrote an article about how we managed that challenge together ("Hip-to-Hip") and Jon wrote at the time: "I am ecstatic about the biking trip. Both of us were really surprised that we could do it. For my 90th birthday, I'm going to ask that my present from Barbara be joining me on a backpacking trip in Alaska (Nah—neither of us likes mosquitoes)".

Jon had officially retired from Harvard Medical School in 2013, but continued to stay involved with his lab and his courses for many years after as a professor emeritus.

THAT TOGETHERNESS we felt on our last bike trip began to fray in 2020, as Jon was diagnosed with Alzheimer's disease. For two years, we coped at home with the help of family, friends, paid companions, a caregivers support group, and his scientific colleagues' "Friends of Jon" WhatsAp group, until trying to keep Jon safe caused me so much stress that I thought I would have a heart attack.

In 2023, Jon moved to the Cadbury Commons' memory care unit in Cambridge, where I continue to take the 15-minute walk to visit him, as do family and friends. It didn't help that in 2022, I fell on the squash court, broke my hip, and needed surgery to secure my upper femur with two metal pins. Or that in 2023, I fell on an uneven concrete sidewalk, injuring my right leg, leading to "fear of falling" anxiety.

Our favorite pastime: hiking in Utah

Women's Writing Workshop, Mission Hill, 2019

12

AND NOW

It is now 2026. I am still writing, mostly personal essays relating to Alzheimer's or to issues around aging, as I seek perspective on both my experience and Jon's (you can read *On Learning to Care: Personal Essays on One Couple's Alzheimer's Experience* and more at www.barbarabeckwith.net). My job life is over, but I continue to feel what I once mused about:

First, let me write.
Let me feel the words slip by. Let me spill them onto the page.
Let writing be my way for a while.
I've been talking a lot.
I've been reading a lot.
I've been thinking a lot.
I've been helpful to people a lot.
I've been traveling a lot.

At one point, I pondered:

But after getting away from writing, I seem to forget how to do it. Does it matter if what I write is good? Does it matter if I keep it or show it to someone, or publish it? Not at this moment.

I want to get back into the stream that's flowing by without me. I want to splash its water in my face, plunge my arms into it, jerk myself awake by it, relax in the cold spots that I would usually try to escape.

I want to write about whatever I would never want to publish, just to feel how it might be different to do so.

As I look back at my life, I see how my passions conflict: I'm an active person, but since writing is my passion, I sit all day. Drafting essays and articles, editing what I've written, reading books—these are the other side of a writer's life.

As a teacher, and later as a reporter, my body was moving all the time. I found time to run and bike and hike and swim. And now age has made even walking perilous (trick knee, icy sidewalks). I walk cautiously, which eliminates my walk's aerobic value. I play piano for relaxation—more sitting.

Back in 2009, when I drafted this "story of my jobs" for Anthony, I ended with this caveat:

I don't feel particularly wise at 72.

In fact, I feel like I have more to learn than to teach.

I haven't been "good" all my life: as a child, I kicked my dog Bonny, down the stairs after he ate my doll; in high school, a boy stole the chem exam and some of us copied it, rationalizing that the just-out-of-grad-school teacher was lousy. In Paris, when we didn't have much money, I took blouses from Au Printemps without paying a few times, desperate to look as good as the Parisians.

Most of my life, my economic leisure has protected me from such temptations.

I am proud of my sons: Ben and Anthony are respectful of women. As a teenager, Anthony said he wouldn't use the word "girlfriend" because "it makes the person seem different from who they really are" and said my feminism "influenced the way I think about things."

Both Ben and Anthony have clear principles but are thoughtful and open to new ideas. They care about "leveling the playing field" re: the world's resources. They lead healthy lives, and balance the job and for-pleasure parts of it: they're as much models for Jon and me as we may be for them. And even though they're on their own, they still enjoy seeing us, their parents!

THIS YEAR, for fun, Anthony and I, who are now "writing buddies," drafted our obituaries. Mine starts: "Barbara Beckwith died on Saturday at age 99, from complications of falling on ice while walking to her neighborhood café for her morning croissant."

I do know I will go, one one way or another, either sooner or later.

Just not yet.

THANKS

This book began its life as something quite different from a memoir: it was simply a list of the jobs that I'd held throughout my life, describing what *I* did and what *I'd* accomplished. But everything I've done in my life has always been more of a *we* than an *I*.

Yes, I mostly write alone, but my ideas emerge from my experiences with others—and those ideas flourish because of the collaboration with, and encouragement of, like-minded people. Same with my teaching, organizing, activism, and anti-racist work. Recognizing other people's contributions to my story is important to me.

I want to thank my writing partner Susan Pollack for offering feedback and encouragement; my life-long friend Jan Gardner, who is always there for me; the White People Challenging Racism co-facilitators and my Social Issues Writing group, who intensified my commitment to racial and equity issues; and the National Writers Union for having my back since 1984.

I am indebted to my relatives and close family members who wrote diaries, letters, and memoirs, allowing me to glimpse into their lives, including my great uncle's Civil War experience, my aunt Ruth's Brooklyn childhood, the story of the daily life of the grandmother, my parents' love letters, and my husband Jon's memoir about his life in science and activism.

Thanks to both Mom and Dad for keeping *my* diaries and letters while Jon and I lived in other cities, states, and countries.

Because I have these writings, I can reconstruct the details my life in a way that's eye-opening—even to myself.

And I need to thank my son Anthony. By encouraging me to write this memoir, he helped me to think through, and find new perspectives on, the past 88 years of my life. It was his brainstorming, editing, book formatting, and cover design that have made the impossible possible. When he was writing his memoir, I mentored him—he has now returned the favor by mentoring me.

Finally, thanks to those who, like me, view the stories of all lives, however they unfold, as worth keeping and sharing.

www.ingramcontent.com/pod-product-compliance
Lightning Source LLC
LaVergne TN
LVHW090523110826
845146LV00003B/960

* 9 7 9 8 9 9 3 1 0 8 7 2 8 *